BRITISH
GARDENS
IN TIME

As seen on BBC
BBC

BRITISH GARDENS IN TIME

THE GREATEST GARDENS AND THE PEOPLE WHO SHAPED THEM

KATIE CAMPBELL

WITH A FOREWORD BY CHRIS BEARDSHAW

F

FRANCES LINCOLN LIMITED
PUBLISHERS

Frances Lincoln Limited
74–77 White Lion Street, London N1 9PF
www.franceslincoln.com

A catalogue record for this book is available
from the British Library.

978-0-7112-3576-2

Printed and bound in Italy

9 8 7 6 5 4 3 2 1

CONTENTS

FOREWORD
BY CHRIS BEARDSHAW

LANDSCAPES AND GARDENS have evolved over the centuries to represent a plethora of philosophies and ideals. From the first expressions of earthly godliness and 'Paradise on Earth' to monumental works of ego; each location feasts off a multitude of stimuli and catalysts.

These artificially crafted and aesthetically responsive gardens are the result of the collision of wealth, peace and confidence, of an individual or a nation. They are often an expression of complex factors in the form of plants, stone, water, pattern and topography, only revealing their significance through the appropriate lens.

Within each garden we can learn much from its history: about the cultural diversity and changes in fashion of ideas and concepts – so many gardens responding to a world enlivened by travel and discovery. Some gardens reveal signs of cultural and artistic trends, their acceptability, interpretation and how they have been implemented. Others display political and philosophical statements heralded in monument and statuary, proclaiming allegiance to long-forgotten causes. Gardens treat us to clear representations of social structure, hierarchical class systems and the aspirations of those with unfolding opportunity and means. Through these gardens we witness fortunes made, inherited and often lost in a relentless desire to carve a statement. All of this is enabled and supported by advances in technology, deployed and harnessed to achieve the garden of one's dreams.

What is often forgotten in any cursory review of these works is that gardens are often modelled in the image of their patron, almost inevitably becoming statements and representations of the individual. As such they serve to inform and enlighten us, perhaps more than any other medium, via four dimensions, on the finer detail and nuances of the personality of the creator.

Perhaps, above all, they are fragile whispers from our ancestors to guide and inspire us in our individual advancement and pursuit of a nature perfected. It is this complexity and tapestry of content that elevates the garden from mere object of art to a running commentary on ourselves. It is also the very point that has tempted and tantalized me about all the gardens I have visited and I hope in this book the gardens draw you into a rewarding dialogue.

Chris Beardshaw
JANUARY 2014

A SHORT HISTORY
OF BRITISH GARDENS

EARLY ROMAN GARDENS

Given that Britain is a country which prides itself on its horticultural prowess, it may come as a shock to discover that the first people to create gardens here were probably the Romans. While the Celts may have encouraged medicinal species to grow near their dwellings, and the Druids had their holy groves, it was the Romans who first made gardens for pleasure. Along with roads, sewers, baths and central heating, the Romans brought their horticultural knowledge to Britain. They also imported their favourite fruits and flowers, introducing to this far-flung colony such scented delights as rosemary, lavender and bay; and supplementing the native plum with cherry, pear and walnut trees. They also managed to acclimatize grapes, all-important for producing the wine that was considered the privilege of every soldier and slave.

Despite such luxuries, those early conquerors were horrified by the new colony. Their expectations were perhaps influenced by stories circulating in Rome since well before the conquest: Ovid believed the Britons painted themselves green, while Pliny the Elder thought they were stained blue; and Horace described them as more remote than anyone else in the world, as well as being very unpleasant to strangers. Julius Caesar, who first visited Britain in 55BC, claimed that nobody would be silly enough to go there except to trade, adding: 'many of the inland Britons do not grow corn. They live on milk and flesh and are clothed in skins.' He did note, however, that while the cattle and trees were of the same varieties as those found in Gaul, the climate was milder. Britain's temperate climate was indeed warmed by the northern extension of the Gulf Stream, and it also allowed the cultivation of a wider range of plants than was possible in the heat of Rome. The first-century historian Tacitus, having complained that 'the sky is foul with incessant rain and clouds', did concede that 'the soil is fertile and bears crops' and that while those crops may germinate late, they shoot up quickly due to 'the terrific dampness of both the land and the air'.

Below: This mural found in Pompeii depicts the Roman fertility figure of Flora, goddess of flowers. Flora was honoured in the 'Floralia', an annual festival held in early spring to celebrate the renewal of life.

Right top: The Romans introduced wine to Britain and cultivated the first vineyards. Winemaking continued after the Roman retreat, especially in the monasteries where wine was essential for celebrating the Eucharist. The Domesday Book of 1086 records forty-six vineyards in southern England, stretching from East Anglia to Somerset; and when Henry VIII ascended the throne in 1509, England had 139 sizeable vineyards.

Right below: The Roman garden at Fishbourne is a modern recreation, although the original bedding trenches, tree pits and post holes were used to determine its layout. Archaeologists discovered these features in the 1960s, despite centuries of ploughing. As few traces of pollen remained to indicate what might have been grown there in the first century, the garden was planted using material described by Pliny and other classical authors.

Even though many Roman sites have been excavated in England, archaeologists have found that remarkably little evidence of gardens has survived. One site that does give a sense of the horticultural achievements of a local ruler (but not of the people he ruled), is the first-century Roman villa at Fishbourne, near Chichester. The palace was a large rectangular building around a central courtyard. This formal space, enclosed by an elegant colonnade, appears to have been embellished with gravel paths, fountains, marble basins, decorative mosaic pavements and low

ANCIENT AND CLASSICAL GARDENS
800BC–AD450

*c.*800BC ANCIENT GREECE
Homer's epic poems *Odyssey* and *Iliad* refer to sacred groves and utilitarian orchards. They also describe palace gardens that appear to be inspired by Persian pleasure gardens.

*c.*400BC CLASSICAL GREECE
There is little evidence of private gardening in classical Greece. Perhaps such signs of personal wealth offended the nascent sense of democracy. The Greeks created sacred shrines embellished with temples, statues, colonnaded walks, grottoes and groves; scholarly academies and gymnasia arose near these shrines and adopted their horticultural accoutrements.

*c.*150BC CONQUERING ROMANS ADOPT GREEK CULTURE
The Romans created pleasure gardens, adopting the elements of Greek sanctuaries without their sacred significance.

AD43 ROMANS INVADE BRITAIN
The Romans introduced horticultural techniques and imported ornamental, culinary and medicinal plants from across a vast empire, creating pleasure gardens as well as utilitarian plantations.

AD410 ROMANS LEAVE BRITAIN
The Romans leave, taking much horticultural knowledge with them.

hedge-lined beds for planting. There is also evidence of an informal garden beyond the palace, with trees, shrubs and streams extending down to the harbour below.

Other sites have yielded more information about plant material. Planting pits discovered in front of the fourth-century Roman villa at Latimer, in Buckinghamshire, probably indicate the position of ornamental trees. At Colchester, mollusc shells suggest that seaweed was used as fertilizer, while carbonized seeds preserved in the soil show the presence of coriander, opium poppy, anise and dill. Excavations at a villa in Silchester, near Reading, reveal that flowers such as roses, violets and aquilegias were grown, along with more utilitarian parsnips, celery, carrots and peas.

Left: This Roman mural from the Villa di Poppaea at Oplontis in Pompeii is typical of the garden scenes that were used to decorate the four walls of a room, creating a virtual indoor garden. Some Romans also ornamented their open courtyards with garden paintings to create the illusion of a larger garden space.

Right (clockwise from top left): Plants such as coriander, dill, violets and opium poppy were used by Romans in Britain. Coriander and dill were culinary herbs, although the Romans also used garlands of dill to crown victorious heroes. Poppies were valued as a narcotic. Violets were used to flavour wine and scent perfume; being among the first plants to flower in spring, they were also associated with rejuvenation and woven into garlands for religious festivals.

MEDIEVAL GARDENS

After the Roman retreat of AD410, and before the Norman invasion of 1066, life in Britain became more primitive and cultivated fields reverted to scrub. The bellicose Anglo-Saxons were unable, or unwilling, to establish peace, which is a prerequisite for the pursuit of gardening; yet Welsh and Saxon law books refer to orchards and vineyards, indicating that viniculture survived. The later Middle Ages were not devoid of luxuries either, as revealed by a late-tenth-century plant list, compiled by Abbot Aelfric of Eynsham. Intended as an aid to teaching Latin, his manuscript gave both Anglo-Saxon and Latin names for hundreds of plants, including peach, pear and fig. Aelfric also lists herbs such as parsley and fennel, whose properties as digestives were valued more than as cooking herbs. Also that century, Bald, a scholar in King Alfred's court, produced his *Leechbook*. Written in the Anglo-Saxon vernacular, this medical text explores many native plants, including the radish, which Bald advocates as a defence against women's chatter: 'taste at night … a root of radish, that day the chatter cannot harm thee.'

Below: Bald's *Leechbook* offered cures for many ills, including chilblains and male impotence. Bottom: The Domesday Book provides a fascinating survey of English medieval life. It was undertaken for William the Conqueror and completed in 1086.

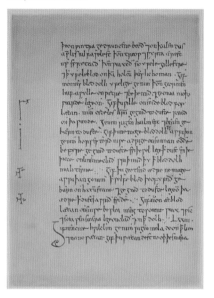

Above: Many early herbals were simply copied, translated, expanded or adapted from previous versions, which led to many inaccuracies. One of the most famous of the early printed herbals was Peter Treveris' *The Grete Herball* of 1526, although it, in turn, was largely derived from a French book.

There is little evidence as to how these vegetables were grown, although the Domesday Book of 1086 makes passing reference to cottagers' gardens. For most villagers, their only garden would have been a patch of earth by the house, where legumes, root vegetables and herbs might be grown to supplement the diet of gruel, bread and ale. Peasants spent their days in the back-breaking cultivation of oats, wheat or barley on strips of land reclaimed from the encroaching forest. Those who ventured out to forage, or take their livestock to graze on the forest floor, had to contend with bears, boar and wolves, beasts which have long since been eradicated.

In 1066, when the Normans conquered Britain, they imposed their harsher 'forest law', confiscating vast tracts of forest to royal ownership, thus depriving the population of a rich, if dangerous, source of food, fuel and timber. Needless to say, courtiers had a different view of forest law from the common people. As royal forests were gradually fenced or walled, embellished with lodges, stocked with deer and improved with new plantings of trees, the joys of the hunt were celebrated in courtly poetry and song. Thought to be the first English hunting manual, *The Master of Game* was written at the beginning of the fifteenth century by Edward of Norwich and reveals a profoundly

400 EARLY CHURCH FATHERS FEAR THAT PAGAN GARDENS WILL LEAD MEN ASTRAY
St Augustine used pagan philosophy to illuminate Christian thought, interpreting gardens symbolically as images of Paradise; plants and other garden features also take on symbolic significance.

800 CHARLEMAGNE BECOMES HOLY ROMAN EMPEROR
In an effort to promote horticultural skills, Charlemagne issued the *Capitulare de Villis* which, among other things, provides a list of 94 plants to be grown in every city in his kingdom.

c.830 ST GALL PLAN
St Benedict recommended gardening as appropriate manual labour for monks; a plan drawn up for the ideal Benedictine monastery included a physic garden, kitchen garden, cellarer's garden, orchard cemetery, cloister garth, green court and private gardens for monks of high office.

1066 NORMAN CONQUEST
England comes under French rule; the reviled King William encloses vast tracts of common land and imposes punitive forest law.

1240 ON THE NATURE OF THINGS, BARTHOLOMEW THE ENGLISHMAN
Bartholomew attempted to organize and catalogue all the knowledge of the day; as well as botany and medicine, his encyclopedia in nineteen books covered astronomy, geography, mineralogy, zoology, philosophy and theology.

Designed to preserve 'venison and vert' – the noble prey and the greenery that sustained it – forest law prohibited such activities as trespass, clearing land, erecting buildings, felling trees, or even taking dogs and certain weapons into the royal forest. By the early thirteenth century, a third of southern England was claimed as royal forest. Any village lying within these boundaries was subject to forest law; and despite the name, royal forest included areas of grass, heath and marshland where game could be found.

Hunting had long been a favourite royal sport. As well as providing respite from the affairs of state and the fetid air of the medieval city, it enabled courtiers to exercise and display their martial skills. More importantly, it allowed the king to demonstrate his power to restive citizens. While the Anglo-Saxon monarchs had been great huntsmen, they had never claimed rights over the forests. 'The Rime of King William', a poem written in 1087, the year of William the Conqueror's death, expresses the widespread resentment felt towards forest law and the harsh penalties dealt out to enforce it – which ranged from fines of varying magnitude to the removal of the offender's eyes, hands or testicles. It is hardly surprising that people like Robin Hood (below), who dared to challenge these laws, have remained folk heroes to this day.

Above: Bartholomaeus Anglicus was a Franciscan monk who wrote an early form of encyclopedia, divided into nineteen books and covering all kinds of subjects, from God and angels, human physiology and animals, to gems, geography, metals, liquids, colour and odour. Along the way it included much on botany and medicine.
Left below: The Celts first exploited the hot springs of Bath, creating a shrine to their goddess Sulis. In around AD60 the Romans constructed a temple to Minerva on the site, and over the next few centuries, established a complex of hot, warm and cold baths. These fell into disrepair after the Roman retreat; but when William the Conqueror's doctor, John of Tours, was made Bishop of Wells, he moved the diocese administration to Bath and made use of the springs' therapeutic powers by restoring the baths and establishing treatment centres. By the late Middle Ages the town had become somewhat decayed, as observed by the sixteenth-century traveller John Leland. While royalty and gentry frolicked in the King's Bath (built over the great bath of Roman times) the poor and diseased were confined to the Cross Bath – where onlookers would gather to jeer at their naked bodies in the foul-smelling waters. In the eighteenth century, the baths were restored once again and Bath became a fashionable spa.

English love of the countryside that endures to this day. While pontificating on such subjects as the etiquette of the sport, the care of hounds, or the nature of harts, hares and wolves, Edward provides a hymn to the natural world: 'For when the hunter riseth in the morning, he sees a sweet and fair morn … and he heareth the song of the small birds … And when the sun is risen, he shall see fresh dew upon the small twigs and grasses … And that is great joy and liking to the hunter's heart.' For the modern reader, such passages could easily obscure the savagery of the hunt itself.

Through these dark and unstable times, monasteries were the main repositories of horticultural knowledge. Many were built on the ruins of old Roman villas, while others adopted the villa form, with buildings arranged around a central, cloistered quadrangle. This interior space was usually laid to grass as the colour green was thought to have therapeutic properties, refreshing the eyes and restoring the minds of monks who perambulated in the shelter of the surrounding cloisters. A central well often embellished these cloister garths, reminding the monks of their Christian duty by its suggestion of purity and baptism. Beyond the garth, most monasteries also contained a medicinal garden attached to the infirmary, and an orchard that doubled as the cemetery – an ideal pairing of symbolism and utility, since the trees that stood for the Garden of Eden would be fertilized by the bodies laid to rest beneath. Monastery gardens usually held fish ponds to supply the Friday fast, and a large, open 'green court' for festivities. The cellarer's garden, under the supervision of the steward, was an important productive space, featuring grapes for the communion wine; hemp and flax to spin into cloth; woad, betony and camomile to use in dyeing; hay for the latrines and rushes for strewing; beehives for honey and candle wax; and vegetables to feed the monks, lay workers, visitors and the ubiquitous poor.

Monks were often the only literate members of the community. They preserved ancient horticultural texts, translating Greek into Latin, and copying them for posterity. Thus endowed with horticultural knowledge that was lost to the rest of the population, monks provided the earliest herbals – catalogues describing plants and their medicinal uses. The first English writer on wider botanical matters was probably the Franciscan monk Bartholomaeus Anglicus – 'Bartholomew the Englishman'. Having studied theology and natural sciences at Oxford University, Bartholomew moved to Germany and in around 1240 wrote *De Proprietatibus Rerum*, meaning *On the nature of things*. Essentially an encyclopedia of science, it covers both medical and botanical knowledge, drawing on the work of Greek, Jewish and Arabic scholars. Having been translated from the original Latin into English in 1398, the book was published in *c.*1495 by means of the newly invented printing press, and became one of the most influential texts of the Middle Ages.

Over the centuries monks experimented with plants and techniques that had been introduced following the Norman Conquest. They used grafting to improve native stock and also received new varieties from their mother houses on the Continent, to supplement the small range of indigenous plants. In the sixteenth century, when Henry VIII destroyed the monasteries and sold off their lands, all trace of these monastic gardens was lost; but by then, the traditions preserved by monks had made their way into the community, for pleasurable and utilitarian ends. The nobles took over wine production, while commoners enjoyed new types of apple, plum and pear.

The idea of a pleasure garden was probably inspired by the Islamic hunting parks and gardens, encountered by courtiers on various Crusades to capture the Holy Land and stem the tide of Muslim expansion. Certainly the menagerie that Henry I built in the early-eleventh century at Woodstock Park – with lions, leopards, porcupines, camels and other exotic animals – has a whiff of the oriental potentate about it. By the twelfth century, England's monarchs were creating private pleasances, which were feminine counterparts to the masculine hunting parks. This horticultural fashion was pioneered by Eleanor of Aquitaine, who introduced French luxury to the English court on her marriage to the future Henry II in 1152. Sadly for Eleanor, the most famous garden of her reign is the bower Henry is said to have made at Woodstock for his mistress, Rosamond Clifford. Legend has it that he created a secret labyrinth deep in the deer park, for the lovers to meet far from the prying eyes of Henry's jealous wife. In the seventeenth century, the antiquarian John Aubrey visited the site and produced a sketch showing an enclosed Islamic-type water garden, with three pools of diminishing size and various pleasure pavilions. Aubrey gives no indication of the legendary labyrinth, nor is there any evidence that Eleanor poisoned Fair Rosamond, although the myth persists. Today nothing remains of that romantic tryst except the aptly named Everswell spring, which once bubbled up in the heart of Rosamond's Bower: it continues to pulse from the rocks, before disappearing

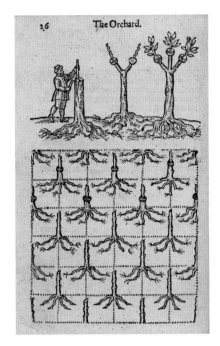

Above: Introduced to Britain by the Romans, the art of grafting was developed by monks during the Middle Ages.
Below: As one of the richest and most powerful women of the Middle Ages, Eleanor of Aquitaine led the fashion for private pleasure gardens.

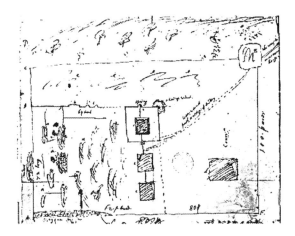

into the lake that Lancelot 'Capability' Brown created five centuries later for Blenheim Palace.

A garden more rooted in history than myth is the one Eleanor created at Winchester Castle. While the current Queen's Garden is a modern recreation, its turf seat, flower beds, wooden pergola and central fountain are all features that would have been found in the pleasure gardens laid out in courtyards, or curtilages, within the ramparts of medieval castles. Planting beds were raised to improve drainage, while gravel paths preserved delicate slippers from dirt. Rose-covered arbours provided shade, essential for ladies' pale complexions, and pergolas offered the possibility of winter exercise. Turf seats were inspired by warmer climes and would have been damp through much of the English summer, but the garden itself, tucked within its high walls, would have offered privacy – a rare commodity in the cramped life of the medieval castle.

Many gardens of the period also had mounds that allowed visitors to see beyond the walls. While these might indicate a precocious desire to draw the wider landscape into the

Above: John Aubrey's sketch of Rosamond's Bower, with three pools. As an amateur archaeologist and pioneer folklorist, Aubrey was enchanted by the legend of Fair Rosamond. The spring at the heart of her garden in Woodstock was said never to run dry, enhancing its reputation for curative powers.
Below: The Queen's Garden at Winchester Castle is a recreation of a medieval garden. It was named after Eleanor of Provence, Henry III's queen, although Eleanor of Aquitaine had a garden here in earlier times.

garden – as became fashionable in the eighteenth century – they were, in fact, designed for surveying the surroundings for potential enemies. At the approach of danger, all horticultural niceties would have been obliterated as local peasants crowded in for safety.

Although no medieval castle gardens remain, images of these early pleasances feature in the illustrations of day books and hymnals created for the aristocracy. While the gardens they depict may represent imaginary as well as real spaces, the purpose of these images was largely metaphorical. The medieval mind, schooled in religious texts, thought in terms of symbolism – and the image of a garden inevitably suggested the *hortus conclusus*, or enclosed garden, of the biblical Song of Songs. A gate evokes the chastity of the Virgin. A fountain indicates purity. A tree alludes to the Edenic tree of knowledge, at the same time prefiguring the Crucifixion cross. Individual flowers also have a story to tell: white and red roses represent the innocence of the Virgin and the blood of her son's sacrifice; carnations, with their flesh-like colour, suggest 'the Word made flesh' and the incarnation of Christ in Mary's womb; lilies denote purity, while ivy, being evergreen, indicates loyalty. The wild strawberries dotting the lawns of many garden images symbolize that perplexing concept: the Virgin Birth. As one of the few plants that flowers and fruits at the same time, strawberries provided an image of purity and fecundity.

The Late Middle Ages was not a propitious time for garden making in England. In the mid-fourteenth century, the temperature of northern Europe fell by an average of 1.5°C/2.4°F, causing crop failure, which led to famine and frequent plagues. The strife of the Hundred Years War, followed by the Wars of the Roses – in which the opposed Houses of York and Lancaster were represented respectively by white and red roses – left little time for horticulture. Remarkably, given the prevailing turmoil, the earliest known

Now was there made fast by the tower's wall
A garden fair, and in the corners set,
A herber green, with wandis long and small
Railed about: and so with trees set
Was all the place, and hawthorn hedges knit,
That not a one was walking there forby
That might within scarce any wight espy.
So thick the boughs and the leaves green
Beshaded all the alleys that there were,
And midst every herber might be seen
The sharp, green, sweet juniper
Growing so fair with branches here and there
That, as it seemed to anyone without,
The boughs spread the herber all about.

Above: This poem was written by James I of Scotland in around 1413, while he was imprisoned in the tower at Windsor Castle. He describes his view of a densely screened pleasure garden set within a corner of the castle wall, where a herber – or arbour – spreads its shade over the lawns. Some words used by the young king might be unfamiliar: 'wandis' (withies), 'forby' (past), 'wight' (living creature).

English gardening manual was produced in the early fifteenth century. *The Feate of Gardening* is a handwritten account in verse by the aptly named Jon Gardener, describing such techniques as sowing, planting and grafting trees. It would be nearly a century before that advice could be properly put into practice, but peace finally blossomed in 1485, when Henry Tudor was crowned Henry VII, married his enemy's daughter and took as his emblem a double, red and white rose. Finally the age of English garden making could begin.

Right: This painting by an unknown German artist of the early fifteenth century is known as *Madonna of the Strawberries*. It shows the Madonna in an enclosed garden, a *hortus conclusus*, which represented chastity in medieval art. The surrounding strawberry plants became an emblem of the Virgin, symbolizing her simultaneous virginity and fecundity because they bear flowers and fruit at the same time. The three-fold form of the strawberry leaf also denotes the Holy Trinity; occasionally the child is depicted holding a strawberry with only two leaflets, the missing third leaflet being the Christ child himself.

TUDOR GARDENS

After all the decades of discord, Henry VII spent his reign consolidating his dynasty and rebuilding his broken country. A frugal man who refrained from pomp and ceremony, his one indulgence was to build Richmond Palace to replace an earlier residence destroyed by fire. It was in this new palace that his son Arthur and Catherine of Aragon celebrated their wedding in 1501. Despite the new ideas about central axes, symmetry and hierarchical ordering of space fermenting on the Continent, this palace looked back to the Middle Ages in both architecture and garden design. An early sixteenth-century visitor noted that the roofs were bristling with pinnacles 'painted and gilt with rich gold and azure', adding that the sound made by the wind passing through these vertical adornments was 'right marvellous'. Henry VII's Groom of the Chamber, Stephen Hawes, wrote a long allegorical love poem entitled 'The Pastime of Pleasure' in which he describes a garden that is believed to be Richmond. The lines 'Rampande lyons stode up wondersly/ Made all of herbes with dulcet swetenes' suggest that the ancient Roman art of topiary was still popular.

Contemporary accounts and later sketches of the garden at Richmond show a low maze, some narrow flower beds and at least one knot – an interlacing geometrical pattern laid out in low, clipped evergreens such as hyssop, germander, lavender or thyme. The space defined by the clipped edging would be filled with sand, crushed brick or coloured gravel for winter interest. Knots were a favourite motif in Tudor carpets, tapestries and fabrics; and although the horticultural knot appears to be a uniquely English phenomenon within the British Isles at this time, its intricate patterns owe something to Celtic design. The garden also contained archery butts, bowling alleys, and raised wooden galleries overlooking the garden that provided cover for winter exercise and indoor games such as chess, dice, billiards and cards. Although clearly designed for pleasure, this is hardly a novel or extravagant garden. Such restraint would not characterize the reign of Henry VII's successor.

As Prince Arthur had died within a year of his marriage, it was his younger brother Henry who became king in 1509. Henry VIII married Arthur's widow and embarked on a grand building programme, in part inspired by the example of his arch-rival King François I of France. On his accession, Henry inherited seven great houses, seventeen lesser houses

Above: Catherine of Aragon (youngest daughter of Ferdinand and Isabella of Spain) was betrothed to Arthur (son of England's Henry VII) when they were both children. They married in 1501, when she was sixteen, but Arthur died six months later. She was betrothed again, this time to Arthur's younger brother Henry, but the marriage was delayed because of disputes between the fathers over Catherine's dowry. When Henry VII died in 1509, Henry VIII immediately married Catherine and had her earlier marriage annulled.

Right top: An engraving of Nonsuch Palace based on a drawing by the Flemish artist Joris Hoefnagel. The most elaborate and expensive of Henry VIII's building projects, Nonsuch was begun in 1538 to celebrate the birth of his son, the future King Edward VI. Sited near one of Henry's hunting grounds in Surrey, it took nine years to complete; over this time Henry's health declined so he could no longer hunt and he rarely visited the palace. It acquired an almost mythical status because of its elegance and opulence, but was destroyed around 150 years later.

Right below: Despite its name, Thornbury Castle is not a true castle. It was designed as a country house rather than a defensive fortress. In 1521, Henry VIII beheaded its owner, his distant cousin Edward Stafford, 3rd Duke of Buckingham, on a trumped-up charge of treason and confiscated the Gloucestershire estate. In 1535 he stayed here for ten days with his short-lived second queen, Anne Boleyn.

and fourteen medieval castles; this number grew to more than sixty by the time he died. Many of these properties, such as Nonsuch – whose very name indicates its desire to be unsurpassed – were fitted with ostentatious gardens designed to dazzle foreign diplomats. Determined to outshine all other nations, Henry also encouraged his courtiers to create grand country estates. But in this, he set them a delicate task: to impress the king without provoking his envy. One of the first to fail was the Duke of Buckingham, who from 1511 transformed his Gloucestershire manor into an elegant rural estate. Known as Thornbury Castle, its lack of real defences indicates the new sense of security during this period.

Thornbury Castle Gloucestershire.
Pub. 25 March 1784 by S. Hooper.

TUDOR GARDENS
1485–1603

1485 HENRY TUDOR WINS THE WARS OF THE ROSES
Henry VII consolidates his kingdom and replenishes the national coffers.

1536–41 DISSOLUTION OF THE MONASTERIES
Henry VIII severs ties with Roman Catholic Pope and sells or gifts lucrative monastic estates to his friends, initiating a fashion for grand country houses and even grander gardens.

1551 WILLIAM TURNER'S HERBAL
The first systematic study of native English plants, written in vernacular English, brings botany to the masses, reflecting the democratizing spirit of the prevailing Protestant mood.

1558 QUEEN ELIZABETH ASCENDS THE THRONE
As she cannot afford to create her own gardens, Elizabeth encourages her courtiers to create lavish gardens in which to entertain her.

1577 DIDYMUS MOUNTAINE, *THE GARDENER'S LABYRINTH*
This early treatise on garden making indicates the growing popularity of pleasure gardens among the rising middle classes.

Left top: Hampton Court Palace had been owned for many years by the Order of St John of Jerusalem before Thomas Wolsey (later appointed cardinal and lord chancellor) took over the site in 1514 and transformed the existing manor house into an elegant, avant-garde palace. With its classical details, rectilinear layout and symmetrical planning, Hampton Court introduced the Italian Renaissance style to England. Wolsey's design forms the heart of the current palace. His outer courtyard, or Base Court, contained lodgings for forty guests; the inner Clock Court contained Wolsey's own private quarters as well as the state apartments reserved for royal visitors. Wolsey's seal still presides over the entrance arch of the clock tower.

Left below: Hampton Court was completed by 1525 and Henry VIII visited soon after. Wolsey had little time to enjoy his palace however, as three years later, aware that he was falling from favour, he gave it to the king. Henry immediately began expanding the palace to accommodate his hundreds of courtiers. Subsequent monarchs continued to reside at Hampton Court until the mid-eighteenth century. The current Privy Gardens reflect the designs of William and Mary, while the Pond Garden (pictured), which today holds a single pond, is thought in Henry's time to have contained several ponds. The beds would have been surrounded by wooden railings painted Tudor green and white.

Right: George Cavendish's *Life of Cardinal Wolsey* includes a poem with these lines describing the secluded knot garden at Hampton Court. As a gentleman in the service of Cardinal Wolsey, Cavendish was required to attend Wolsey at all times. He became a close confidant of the cardinal, and his biography is one of the few authentic records of the divorce proceedings against Catherine of Aragon, as well as being an important source of information on court life under Henry VIII. After the Cardinal's death in 1530 Cavendish retired from court life.

Contemporary accounts praise the large windowed galleries overlooking the garden, with its orchard full of newly grafted trees, 'goodly alleys' and 'many roses and other pleasures'. The windows and galleries remain to this day, although the castle was left unfinished because in 1521 Buckingham was beheaded on a trumped-up charge of treason, in part because his overweening extravagance offended the king.

Even more dramatic was the case of Cardinal Wolsey; thought to be the son of an Ipswich butcher, he rose through the treacherous Tudor court to become Henry's chief minister. As the king indulged in an endless round of hunts, fetes, tilts and masquerades, Wolsey was left to run the country. With his financial rewards, Wolsey created grand residences for himself at York House in central London and at Hampton Court, several miles south-west along the river Thames. These estates begin to reflect the new design ideas evolving in Italy – ideas that Wolsey would have seen at first hand while on diplomatic missions abroad. From the mid-fifteenth century, the humanist philosophers of Renaissance Italy had begun to celebrate nature, extolling the health, purity and delight of rural life. Architects soon followed, tearing down defensive outer walls to open up to the wider landscape, establishing logical links between dwelling and garden with central axes, symmetrical beds and room-like enclosures ornamented with sculptures inspired by figures from classical mythology.

England's garden style may have evolved more quickly had Wolsey remained in power long enough to promote these Renaissance concepts. But in 1530, when he failed to secure the papal annulment that would allow Henry to remarry, the king confiscated his properties and accused him of treason

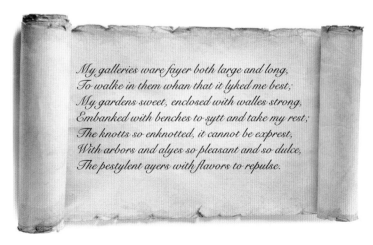

My galleries ware fayer both large and long,
To walke in them whan that it lyked me best;
My gardens sweet, enclosed with walles strong,
Embanked with benches to sytt and take my rest;
The knotts so enknotted, it cannot be exprest,
With arbors and alyes so pleasant and so dulce,
The pestylent ayers with flavors to repulse.

— Wolsey died on the way to trial. Shakespeare's *Henry VIII* describes this sudden fall from favour by using richly ironical horticultural metaphors, depicting Wolsey as a fine fruit tree laden with 'blushing honours', whose greatness is 'ripening' when a sudden 'killing frost' destroys his roots.

With the cardinal gone, the king moved his family into York House – renaming it Whitehall Palace – but focused his attentions on Hampton Court. Having broken with Rome and declared himself head of the Church in England, Henry began transforming his estates to provide a setting that would match his new, self-proclaimed status. Despite their vast scale and obvious grandeur, his gardens remained more medieval than Renaissance in style. He expanded the grounds at Hampton Court and created a Privy Garden beneath the royal apartments for Anne Boleyn, his queen from 1533 to 1536. There were flower beds ornamented with traditional English knots also, covered arbours, raised turf walks, a great many sundials – attesting to the king's

Above: These early-sixteenth-century figures, the Dacre Beasts, are rare examples of the Tudor tradition of heraldic ornament, and similar to the sculptures that would have adorned Henry VIII's Privy Garden. Carved from the trunk of a single oak tree, they represent a gryphon, ram, dolphin and bull – emblems of the Dacre family, one of the most powerful dynasties in Tudor England.

ENCLOSURE MOVEMENT EVICTS PEASANTS FROM THE LAND

During Henry VIII's reign (1509–1547) the population grew by 25 per cent, stretching England's ability to feed her own people. Resources were put under further pressure by the growth in the wool trade. With English wool commanding high prices at home and abroad, landowners began to shift from arable farming to sheep production (romantically portrayed in this engraving, right). As farmers turned their fields over to pasture, tenants were evicted because their labour was no longer needed, subsistence farmers were forced to sell to larger, more profitable enterprises and common land was enclosed to make it private property – depriving peasants of ancient rights held under the earlier open-field system of strip farming. Enclosure had begun in the twelfth century, but intensified in Tudor times and reached its height in the eighteenth century. As early as 1516 Sir Thomas More deplored the practice, noting in his *Utopia*:

The increase in pasture . . . by which your sheep, which are naturally mild, and easily kept in order, may be said now to devour men and unpeople, not only villages, but towns; for wherever it is found that the sheep of any soil yield a softer and richer wool than ordinary, there the nobility and gentry, and even those holy men, the abbots not contented with the old rents which their farms yielded, nor thinking it enough that they, living at their ease, do no good to the public, resolve to do it hurt instead of good. They stop the course of agriculture, destroying houses and towns, reserving only the churches, and enclose grounds that they may lodge their sheep in them.

interest in science – and some extravagant topiary. Nearby a grand mount, with a path winding up to a banqueting house, was crowned with a magnificent gilded dome.

Eschewing the Italian fashion for classical statuary, Henry chose to celebrate his own lineage by placing sculptures of heraldic beasts in the Privy Garden. The flower beds were enclosed by edging rails painted Tudor green and white, and punctuated with rows of carved wooden lions, dragons, greyhounds, antelopes and other animals drawn from medieval heraldry. These suggested an ancient heritage for the fledgling Tudor dynasty, and were adjusted as one royal bride gave way to another: the Boleyn falcons and leopards being replaced by Seymour panthers and unicorns. Standing some 2.5 metres/8 feet high on their painted posts – higher still with crests depicting the royal arms – the beasts must have presented a bizarre and terrifying spectacle to visitors approaching by river. For while Henry may have looked to the past to inspire his gardens, as a master of propaganda he transformed the English royal garden from a place of domestic pleasure into a setting for dynastic display.

ELIZABETHAN GARDENS

Despite all his bluff and extravagance, when Henry VIII died in 1547 he left his kingdom in turmoil, virtually bankrupt and torn by religious dissent. When Elizabeth eventually inherited the throne in 1558 she had neither the desire nor the funds to indulge in grand building projects; instead, she encouraged her courtiers to do this for her. Over the course of her father's reign gardening had become a symbol of prestige, a way for ambitious men to demonstrate their wealth and sophistication. This impetus was heightened by plants coming in from the newly discovered Americas, as well as ideas brought back from other countries by scholars, merchants and diplomats. When England embraced the Protestant religion and relations with the Catholic south became strained, English travellers maintained lively links with northern Europe. Advice for the novice gardener appeared in the form of small, illustrated books that were relatively cheap to produce, due to the invention of the printing press. In 1533 John Fitzherbert published his *Book of Husbandry*, which includes digressions on such genteel subjects as prodigality, religion, the breeding of horses and the selling of timber. Clearly the work of a country gentleman rather than a mere farmer, Fitzherbert's book demonstrates how gentrified country life had become.

More practical in content was the *Most Brief and Pleasant Treatise* published in 1558 by an enterprising astrologer, translator and writer named Thomas Hill. Capitalizing on the vogue for garden making, Hill's convenient, pocket-sized manual taught the new land-owning classes 'how to dresse, sowe, and set a garden'. As the first book was devoted specifically to the English garden, the *Treatise* was extremely popular; its success was also due to Hill's enthusiasm and informal tone, as well as his detailed advice on such mundane issues as choosing a site, preparing beds and dealing with slugs and snails. So popular was the book that it went into at least seven further editions, for which Hill invented various new titles. His final book, *The Gardener's Labyrinth*, appeared in 1577, after his death, and was published under the pseudonym Didymus Mountaine (a play on Hill's name). It was extremely successful, not least because of the delightful illustrations that combine narrative humour with practical instruction. Presenting the medical benefits of 'ech herb, plant and floure' he explains, for example, that distilled water of borage 'removeth melancholie' while

bugloss 'prevaileth for the roughnesse of the throat and cough'. He also promotes the idea of making simple flower gardens, a suggestion which his countrymen embraced with zeal.

Like her father before her, Elizabeth cleverly exploited the symbolism of the garden. Tainted by the slur of illegitimacy, she positioned herself as a modest, virginal English flower. Shifting focus from the Tudor rose of her ancestors to her own chosen emblem of the eglantine, or common sweet briar, Elizabeth placed herself at the heart of the humblest garden – the first people's queen. This garden imagery was duly adopted by writers and artists. Shakespeare's John of Gaunt in *Richard II* describes England as an Eden and demi-paradise before his famous line: 'This blessed plot, this earth, this realm, this England'. The court painter Isaac Oliver portrayed the queen, then in her seventh decade, decked in a gown of English wild flowers in the guise of Astraea, the wise virgin of Virgil's fourth eclogue, who ushers in the Golden Age where nature freely gives her bounty. Indeed, during Elizabeth's reign garden imagery flourished as queen, country, garden, flowers, chastity and fecundity all became entwined in a tangle of royal allegory, which appears to be an attempt by the Protestant monarch to usurp the Catholic imagery of the Virgin Mary.

Although Elizabeth made no gardens for herself, aspiring courtiers adopted the fashionable new Renaissance principles for their grand gardens, created in the hope of enticing her to visit. While lacking the steep terraced sites and strict symmetry of the Italian originals, these gardens nevertheless gave an impression of order – with the house in the centre of the design like the queen in the heart of her kingdom. The kitchen garden would be sited on the service side of the house, and the south side would preferably be reserved for pleasure grounds. These would be overlooked by the main reception rooms and accessed by a raised terrace from which their geometric patterns could be appreciated. Flights of steps, wide walks and smaller ancillary paths would connect the various parts of the garden, which might include orchards, fountains,

Below: A dusting of frost emphasizes the planting pattern in this Elizabethan-style knot garden. Like the ornate patterns on Elizabethan lace, fabric and ceiling bosses, knot gardens were fussy and ordered. Aromatic and culinary herbs such as marjoram, thyme and lemon balm were often used to define the outline, with the spaces in between picked out by a layer of coloured sand, powdered brick or gravel.

knots and mazes, arbours and rose gardens. The forests from which these estates were carved were often fenced to a point just beyond the front gate; this provided a deer park, and became the space that developed into the landscape park of the eighteenth century.

The stories surrounding the gardens of Elizabethan courtiers are the stuff of fiction. Nonsuch had been Henry VIII's grandest building project, taking nine years to build, yet he visited it only three times and the garden was unfinished when he died. It was put up for sale and purchased by the Earl of Arundel in a bid to woo Elizabeth. Arundel then bankrupted himself restoring the gardens to Henry's original plan. When Elizabeth rejected his suit, the earl conspired with fellow Catholics to have her replaced by Lady Catherine Grey, sister of the short-lived Lady Jane. He was put under house arrest and eventually the estate passed to his son-in-law, Lord Lumley, who gifted it back to the queen but stayed on as its guardian. To atone for his part in his father-in-law's treachery, Lumley spent the rest of his life developing the gardens as an elaborate allegory. In a novel horticultural move, he set his Diana Grove in a 'wilderness'; this informal planting of trees – one of the first to be laid out in England – indicates a precocious desire for respite from the surrounding formality. Celebrating Elizabeth as the goddess Diana, Lumley cast himself as the hapless Actaeon, who stumbles upon the deity bathing naked in a pool, is transformed into a stag and savaged

NONSUCH: AN UNPARALLELED AFTERLIFE

In 1582, Anthony Watson provided a detailed and obsequious account of Nonsuch gardens, dedicated to Lord Lumley to whom he owed his position as Rector of Cheam. Watson describes a theatrical ensemble of fruit trees, evergreens, ferns, shrubs and vines; in the midst of these stood a group of stone deer, horses, rabbits and dogs which appeared to be giving chase and running over the grass. In 1600, Baron Waldstein extolled Nonsuch's gardens and groves, declaring them to be 'the finest in the whole of England'. Provoked perhaps by the hubris inherent in the name Nonsuch, the English Civil War wreaked havoc on the estate. In 1665, sixteen years after the Civil War had ended,

Samuel Pepys was visiting the Treasury – which had moved its offices to rural Nonsuch to avoid the plague in central London – and records in his diary: '... walked in the ruined garden'. The following year, John Evelyn bemoaned the state of its royal forest, 'felled by those destructive and avaricious rebels in the late war which defaced one of the stateliest seats his Majesty had'. The *coup de grâce* came when Charles II gave Nonsuch to his favourite mistress, Barbara Villiers. Keen to raise funds to pay off her gambling debts, she demolished the palace to sell the building materials; a little while later, and much more profitably, she sold off the parks.

by his own dogs. Although the association was intended to flatter the queen with its suggestion of her divine chastity and wisdom, Elizabeth was, in fact, a keen huntress. Unlike most women of her time, who would watch the hunt from rooftops or specially constructed pavilions, Elizabeth rode with the hounds and was present at the kill.

Another unsuccessful suitor for the queen's hand was Sir Christopher Hatton, Elizabeth's lord chancellor and one of her favourite ministers. Like the Earl of Arundel, Hatton bankrupted himself creating Holdenby House in Northamptonshire. With a long front drive, two great courtyards, terraces, rose garden, orchard, pond, mount and grand banqueting house, the ensemble was so opulent that Ben Jonson used it as a symbol of the extravagance and corruption of the Elizabethan court. Hatton vowed not to spend a night in the house until his monarch visited, but he died in 1591 and Elizabeth never set foot in the place. Another important minister, William Cecil Lord Burghley, fared better; his house Theobalds, in Hertfordshire, being more accessible from London and close to the great hunting parks of Enfield and Waltham Forest, was graced with many a royal visit. Although the original house and gardens

Above: Theobalds demonstrated Lord Burghley's growing wealth, sophistication and influence at court, and was created with the purpose of enticing Queen Elizabeth to visit. The formal gardens were inspired by Italian and French examples, and England's foremost botanist, John Gerard, acted as their superintendent. Burghley's gamble paid off handsomely, as the queen graced Theobalds with no fewer than eight royal visits.

have disappeared, archival sketches and a description by Paul Hentzner, a German lawyer who journeyed through England in the late sixteenth century, depict several grand outer courtyards and an elaborate garden that was surrounded by a moat furnished with pleasure boats.

Burghley's great rival for the queen's affections, if not her hand, was Robert Dudley, Earl of Leicester, who transformed the medieval castle of Kenilworth into a fairyland for a nineteen-day visit by the queen in 1575. Between the whirl of masques, hunts, fireworks, dances, concerts and picnics, the queen would retire to the garden he created beneath her apartments. Robert Laneham, a minor court official, described a wide, high terrace, overlooking a rectangular space bisected by paths – which some thought were paved in gold because of their glittering sand. Flanked by rose-covered arbours, and backed by a gilded aviary, the central space held four flower-filled parterres around a central Atlas fountain. Laneham compares the garden to Paradise, suggesting that if it lacks 'the fair rivers', it is all the better for not possessing the 'unhappy' tree of knowledge. The serpent was waiting, however, probably in the form of Lord Burghley, who is rumoured to have warned Elizabeth that her lady-in-waiting, Lettice Knollys, Countess of Essex, was pregnant by Dudley. The countess was banished forever from court, Dudley relinquished all hopes of a royal marriage and the garden was left to neglect and decay. Although it has recently been restored by English Heritage, the flimsiness of the materials and the simplicity of the design suggest

Below: This is a garden scene from Kenilworth today. Having gifted Kenilworth to her favourite courtier, Robert Dudley, Earl of Leicester, the queen visited this distant estate several times on her summer progresses from London. Her fourth and final visit lasted nineteen days, the longest time Elizabeth had ever stayed with a courtier. Dudley furnished grand apartments for the queen's exclusive use, with large windows overlooking the intimate Privy Garden he had created for her visit.

that the garden was probably intended to be impermanent – like the court masques, procession banners and even the queen's affection. In his 1577 account *A Description of England*, William Harrison, canon of Windsor, celebrates the improvements seen in horticulture over the past four decades. Noting that plants were arriving from such far-flung places as India, Ceylon and the Americas, he decries the gardens of the past as 'but dunghills and laystows [open drains]' compared with the glories of the present day. Within a few years these open, floral gardens would be swept away in the fascination with opulence and drama ushered in by the extravagant King James I, whose accession to the English throne in 1603 marked the end of the Tudor dynasty.

Right: In his Holborn garden John Gerard cultivated many exotic plants introduced from the New World. His famous *Herball* of 1597 was largely translated from a herbal by the Flemish botanist Rembert Dodoens, while its woodcut illustrations came from sixteenth-century Dutch botanical texts. Gerard's *Herball* was dedicated to Lord Burghley.

HERBALS BECOME BESTSELLERS

While herbals were among the most popular books of the sixteenth and early-seventeenth centuries, they fell from favour with the rise of more scientific approaches to pharmacology. In 1551, the English cleric and physician William Turner published his *New Herball*. Written in the vernacular tongue and accompanied by clear woodcut images, this three-volume work was the first systematic study of a wide range of English plants, enabling the reader to find, identify and exploit 'the uses and virtues' – or properties – of 238 native species. A 'herb' at that time meant any useful plant, including such material as the silver birch: 'greatly fearful to many because the offyceres make roddes of it'; or wood sorrel, which makes a good green sauce to whet the appetite, and is known as Alleluia, 'because it appeareth about Easter when Alleluia is sung again'.

In his introduction Turner admits that some may condemn him for revealing professional secrets, but his determination to educate and empower ordinary people reflects his strong Protestant values. In 1551 Turner was appointed Dean of Wells, but two years later, with the accession of the Catholic Queen Mary, his books were banned and he was forced into exile. Elizabeth restored him, but in 1564 he was suspended once again for nonconformity. By contrast, John Gerard's much more famous 1597 *Herball* was little more than a translation of an earlier Dutch work, with a few additions from his own garden. Today Gerard remains a favourite, largely for the charm of his prose with its beguiling folk names like 'Herb Impious', 'Ladies' Cushion' or 'Go-to-bed-at-Noon'.

Below: This is probably the earliest printed map of London, and is known as *Civitas Londinium* or the Agas Map after Ralph Agas, a sixteenth-century English surveyor famed for his plans of Oxford, Cambridge and London – although there is some dispute as to whether Agas was, in fact, the work's creator. Produced from eight wooden blocks, it is over 1.8 metres/6 feet long and 60cm/2 feet wide. With its bird's-eye view, which shifts to panorama as it rises to the north, the map provides a comprehensive image of London's sixteenth-century streets and buildings.

Bottom: The rich narrative detail of the *Civitas Londinium* offers a fascinating insight into the life of Tudor London, for example showing windmills, archers and laundresses in Finsbury Fields outside the city wall to the north, and formal gardens in the densely populated districts within.

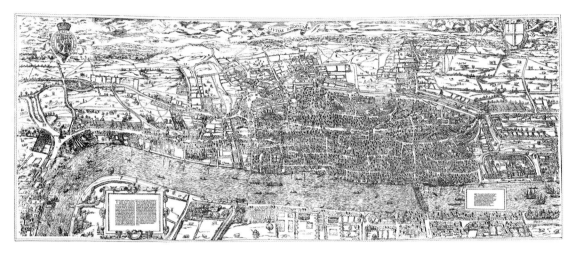

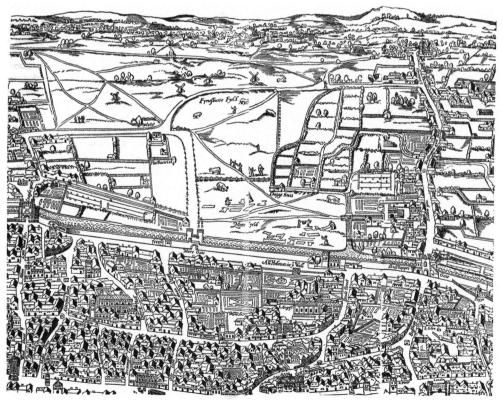

JACOBEAN GARDENS

In the early seventeenth century, England became increasingly urbanized and cosmopolitan as links with continental Europe were strengthened, the first British colonies were founded in North America and trade was established with India. King James I's court was known for its luxury and extravagance. The king was fond of elaborate entertainments and drama prospered. Jacobean gardens became grander and iconography shifted from Tudor heraldry to classical mythology, as sculpture, fountains and grottoes became fashionable.

Whereas sixteenth-century horticulture had been shaped by the simple geometries of the Italian Renaissance, seventeenth-century gardens were dominated by the absolutist ideas of the French court. Great canals, grand tree-lined avenues and endless, scrollwork parterres replaced enclosed courtyards and clipped herbal knots. Fascinated by science, King James imported continental architects and engineers such as Isaac and Salomon de Caus. When Salomon de Caus remodelled Somerset House, he created a

Below: The French architect Isaac de Caus began laying out the garden at Wilton House in the early 1630s. As one of the first French-style parterre gardens in England, it was considered novel at the time. In the mid-1640s de Caus secured the garden's fame by publishing an illustrated description entitled *Le Jardin de Wilton*. The garden became extremely influential at the time of the restoration of the monarch in 1660 when, following the austerity of the Commonwealth period, grand gardens became fashionable again.

Right below: The childhood home of several of Henry VIII's children, the Old Palace at Hatfield was Elizabeth I's favourite residence. Her successor James I preferred Theobalds, a more stylish building then owned by his chief minister and William Cecil's son, Robert Cecil, and insisted on swapping houses. Relocated, Cecil tore down three wings of the king's old palace and used the bricks to build the current Hatfield House. Little of the sumptuous garden he created around his new dwelling has survived: this parterre beside the house was laid out in the twentieth century.

large, patterned parterre and an elaborate fountain-grotto representing Mount Parnassus. Salomon's brother Isaac created a famous garden for the 4th Earl of Pembroke at Wilton House, in Wiltshire. Here, a large, walled enclosure was divided by a broad central path leading past four ornate, symmetrical parterres filled with classical statuary. The rustic grotto at the end of the path displayed de Caus's talent for hydraulics and automata; the spouts and jets were still working in the 1680s, when seen by the indomitable traveller Celia Fiennes during her tour of England on horseback. She delighted in the figures that could weep water on the beholders, and other devices that made the sound of birdsong.

Meanwhile, James I was so impressed by Lord Burghley's garden at Theobalds, in Hertfordshire, that he invited Burghley's son, Robert Cecil, to give it to him in exchange for his own palace at Hatfield. Cecil had little choice but to concede. He consoled himself by taking his father's gardener, Mountain Jennings, and creating an even grander garden at Hatfield. He engaged Salomon de Caus to design a diamond-shaped lake with an island furnished with mounts, pavilions and a banqueting house. The grounds were further embellished with orchards of white figs, peaches, nectarines, oranges and pomegranates supplied by John Tradescant, an intrepid plant collector who traversed

STUART GARDENS
1603–1688

1603 JAMES STUART BECOMES KING OF ENGLAND
As links with Europe open up, French and Italian influence is seen in the popularity of such garden features as grottoes, groves, fountains and classical statuary.

1615 PURITAN EXPANSION
Gervase Markham's *The English Hus-wife: containing the inward and outward Vertues which ought to be in a complete woman*. In the early seventeenth century, Puritan pieties infuse all aspects of life, including gardens.

1621 OXFORD PHYSIC GARDEN
The founding of England's first botanic garden reflects the growing interest in the natural sciences. During the Commonwealth (1649–1660) opulent gardens were frowned upon, but scientific or utilitarian horticulture was encouraged.

1664 JOHN EVELYN'S *SYLVA, OR A DISCOURSE OF FOREST-TREES*
Distressed by the destruction of aristocratic forests and formal avenues during the Commonwealth, John Evelyn advocated tree planting as an act of patriotism, to replenish the supply of oaks needed to build ships for Britain's navy.

1681 BROMPTON PARK NURSERY
Founded by George London and Henry Wise, this nursery catered to the taste for grand formal gardens promoted by Charles II on his return from exile in France in 1660.

Europe from Russia to the Levant. Tradescant became famous for the collection of natural curiosities at his south London home, The Ark. He and his son, also John, introduced many plants to Britain, and the genus *Tradescantia* is named in their honour. In 1625, the year of James I's death, Sir Francis Bacon, philosopher, scientist and statesman, penned his famous essay 'Of Gardens'. He described garden making as the purest of human pleasures, 'without which, buildings and palaces are but gross handiworks'. Bacon saw gardens as an important art form, to be experienced with all five senses.

Right: John Tradescant the Elder began his career as head gardener to Robert Cecil at Hatfield House. In 1611 Cecil sent Tradescant to the Low Countries to buy varieties of fruit trees for his new garden.
Below (left and right): Blue-flowered *Tradescantia* was named in honour of Tradescant and his botanist son, who brought back the tulip tree and other plants from his voyages in America.
Opposite: Sir Francis Bacon's work led to the modern scientific method. He made a garden in Hertfordshire and wrote about the pleasure it gave him.

CAROLINE AND
COMMONWEALTH GARDENS

With the accession of Charles I to the throne in 1625, the Gallic influence on gardens continued. Charles' French wife Henrietta Maria employed French garden designer André Mollet to improve the royal gardens. By means of the *patte d'oie*, Mollet adapted the tree-lined *allées* typical of French royal gardens to England's more hilly topography. These three-pronged paths radiating from the same point offered shorter avenues, fit more for walking than hunting; they also provided a variety of views out to the park and in towards the house.

During the time of Commonwealth (1649–1660) even such reduced grandeur was frowned upon. Many aristocrats discreetly retreated to their rural estates. Since luxury and ostentation were condemned as royal vices, they tended to focus on agriculture rather than horticulture. However, at the other end of the social scale gardening became politically charged. In 1649 the Diggers, a small revolutionary group, declared that property was essentially theft. Occupying common land on St George's Hill, Surrey, they set up camp, planted vegetables and invited the local population to join them in pulling down the enclosures (see page 25). Needless to say, the local landowners soon put a stop to such idealistic activities.

The systematic study of plants had been stimulated by the founding of Oxford Botanic Garden in 1621, and under Cromwell's puritanical rule the Jacobean fascination with science was channelled towards practical ends, leading to great improvements in agricultural productivity. With the aim of helping the poor feed themselves, Ralph Austen, an Oxford nurseryman, suggested a national programme for planting fruit trees, detailed in his *Treatise* of 1653. Under the Commonwealth, commoners had vindictively destroyed the grand avenues, elite hunting forests and commercial woodlands of the aristocracy. England's forests were also being stripped of trees during the seventeenth century to fuel the furnaces of the early Industrial Revolution. So grave was this deforestation that, in 1664, the great diarist and arboriculturist John Evelyn published his *Sylva* (see page 35) advising landowners on the techniques and benefits of reforestation.

The Restoration of Charles II in 1660 reintroduced autocratic formality to the English garden. Mollet returned,

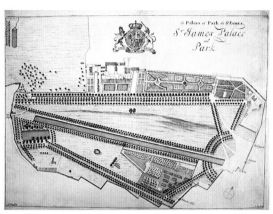

Above: This early eighteenth-century view of St James's Park is Johannes Kip's engraving of a painting by Leonard Knyff. Charles II had been impressed by the elaborate French parks that he had seen while in exile on the Continent, so after his Restoration he summoned André Mollet to redesign St James's in the grand formal style. Mollet was a French garden designer who worked for several royal clients, including Charles' father and Queen Christina of Sweden. His most notable addition at St James's is the long canal which he laid diagonally through the park.

Right: Ralph Austen's book, *A Treatise of Fruit-Trees*. The frontispiece image refers to the enclosed garden celebrated in the biblical Song of Songs, which itself symbolizes the Church. Like many fellow Calvinists, Austen saw a spiritual as well as a practical benefit in cultivating the earth; he went so far as to suggest that trees were books in which God's attributes could be read. This heavily theological approach hindered the sale of his *Treatise*, although it remains a most detailed and readable account of arboriculture.

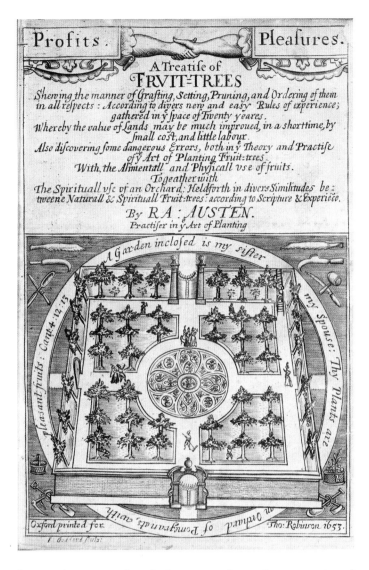

having disappeared with the monarchy, and was appointed keeper of the royal gardens at St James's Park. Here he laid out long, tree-lined avenues and an endless canal – a fitting playground for the pelicans given to the king by the Russian ambassador in 1666. The park was also playground to the monarch's less reputable friends; it was here that he would entertain such favourites as actress Nell Gwyn and the rakish poet John Wilmot, 2nd Earl of Rochester. Before his death from venereal disease at the age of thirty-three, Rochester penned a gloriously bawdy paean to promiscuity, 'A Ramble in St James's Park'. This cheerful catalogue of sexual transgressions reveals the social permeability of the royal grounds at night.

Mollet died in 1665 and was replaced as royal gardener by John Rose, who studied under Le Nôtre in France. A master of viniculture, his *The English Vineyard Vindicated* (1666) was a standard work on the subject, although he is remembered principally, but erroneously, for producing

Unto this all-sin-sheltering grove
Whores of the bulk and the alcove,
Great ladies, chambermaids, and drudges,
The ragpicker, and heiress trudges.
Carmen, divines, great lords, and tailors,
Prentices, poets, pimps, and jailers,
Footmen, fine fops do here arrive,
And here promiscuously they swive . . .

Above: The pelicans here in St James's Park recall the pair of pelicans given to Charles II by the Russian ambassador in the 1660s. Although viewed as a source of competition by fishermen, in the seventeenth century pelicans would have been a suitable royal gift because they symbolize sacrifice and Christ's Passion – it being thought that the birds pierce their own breasts to feed their young with drops of blood. Elizabeth I adopted the pelican to suggest her role as mother of the Church of England. James I had an image of a pelican feeding its young placed on the title page of the first edition of his King James Bible.

Left: An excerpt from the Earl of Rochester's deliciously bawdy poem, 'A Ramble in St James's Park'. Originally, the park was designed to recreate the purity of the countryside in an urban setting – Henry VIII acquired it as a deer park and Elizabeth I held pastoral fetes in its meadows. However, under Charles II it was opened to the public and soon became nortorious as a place of sexual depravity.

Above: In this painting by Hendrick Danckerts, the royal gardener John Rose presents a pineapple to King Charles II. The ability to grow pineapples was a sign of the patron's wealth as it demanded a 'stove' or heated greenhouse; it was also a sign of the gardener's prowess, as fumes from the furnace could easily destroy the fruit.

England's first pineapple. In fact, like many English gardeners of the time, he simply ripened fruit from mature stock imported from Europe or the West Indies.

In the Glorious Revolution of 1688, Mary and her Dutch husband William of Orange were crowned joint monarchs, replacing the Stuart dynasty and ushering in a more relaxed, republican style of government. Dutch gardens tended to be smaller than their European counterparts; and while order and symmetry were valued, detail counted more than scale. The Dutch canalized drainage ditches to create rectangular pools; they preferred low coniferous cones and spherical topiary to grand tree-lined avenues, and the flat plains of the Netherlands had little need for the viewing platforms, great staircases or elaborate terracing of traditional Renaissance gardens. As these more modest traditions took root in England, intricate French parterres gave way to simple Dutch grass squares – and the English began their obsession with the lawn. At the time, however, the Dutch were the greatest traders in the world, so exotic new plants poured in from the Orient, India and the Americas. The King was

keen on floral shrubs, known as 'greens', which had to be kept under cover in winter. This gave rise to the fashion for 'green houses', which courtiers filled with tubs of clipped orange trees in homage to their monarch, William of Orange.

After moving to Britain, the asthmatic king soon discovered he could not abide the smoky air of central London, so the royal couple moved out to rural Kensington and commissioned Sir Christopher Wren to transform an old Jacobean mansion into a comfortable palace. To ensure safe passage from his offices in Whitehall, William created a private road flanked by 300 oil lamps. Known initially as the Rue du Roi, its name was soon corrupted into Rotten Row, but it remains to this day as a broad, sandy bridleway traversing the south side of Hyde Park. Queen Mary, meanwhile, hired George London and Henry Wise to create a garden for her new abode. From their 40-hectare/100-acre Brompton Park Nursery nearby, this famous duo supplied all sorts of trees, shrubs and flowers – along with the designs to absorb them. George London had studied under John Rose and, while their speciality was creating grand gardens for lesser mortals, the team worked on various royal palaces as well as such grand estates as Longleat, Badminton, Chatsworth and Blenheim. From their stock of 40,000 plants London and Wise could offer some 70 varieties of pear; but the royal

Above: A Dutch greenhouse. William and Mary were both passionate collectors of rare plants. In the Netherlands, and later in England, their precious cacti, yuccas, aloes, palms, citruses and other exotics were protected from the northern winter in hothouses and orangeries. While mundane plants might be grown in wooden tubs, the rarest and most prized plants were kept in ornate clay pots often elaborately decorated, glazed or even gilded. These were transported outside to display in the garden for the summer months. By the late seventeenth century William and Mary's botanical collection at Hampton Court was one of the finest in the world, with over 2,000 species. Their 1,000 orange trees were particularly prized since the orange was a symbol of William's dynasty, the House of Orange.

tastes, in this republican age, were diplomatically restrained. A visitor to the garden in the autumn of 1691 observed: "Kensington Gardens are not great nor abounding with fine plants. The orange, lemon, myrtles and what other trees they had there in summer were all removed to Mr London's and Mr Wise's greenhouse at Brompton Park, a little mile from them. But the walks and grass are laid very fine and they were digging up a flat of four or five acres to enlarge their gardens".

Above: The engraving of Kensington Palace from Kip and Knyff's seminal *Britannia Illustrata* (1707) indicates that, although the garden retained the broad central walk and symmetrical layout of earlier baroque designs, its modest, domestic scale, scrollwork parterres, low hedging, brightly coloured flowers and neatly clipped topiary cones were typical of the new Dutch style.

Below: A prolific writer, garden designer and nurseryman, Stephen Switzer was also an early advocate of naturalistic planting. He audaciously asserted in his 1718 work *Ichnographia Rustica*: 'If the beauties of nature were not corrupted by art, gardens would be much more valuable.'

Towards the end of the seventeenth century even these modest formalities were deemed too restrictive. In his book *Upon the Gardens of Epicurus* (1685) the diplomat Sir William Temple was one of the first to push for a looser, more natural garden style. Inspired by the patterns on Chinese porcelain, he advocated sinuous lines and sensuous forms, using the term 'sharawadgi' – possibly based on the Japanese *sorowaji*, meaning asymmetry. In 1712 Joseph Addison, in the newly formed *Spectator* magazine, went further and actually ridiculed contemporary tastes. Claiming he would rather see a natural tree 'in all its luxuriancy and diffusion of boughs' than the unnatural topiary cones and globes which were then the height of fashion, he considered that 'an orchard in flower looks infinitely more delightful than all the little labyrinths of the most finished parterre.'

Soon the debate was joined by the influential critic Stephen Switzer, who rose from jobbing gardener to become foreman at the Brompton Park Nursery. In his *Ichnographia Rustica* (1715), Switzer argued against his own commercial interests when he asked: '*Why should we be at the great expense of levelling hills or filling up of dales when they are the beauty of nature?*'

This innocent question spelt the end of three centuries of formal gardening, and the great English landscape style was born. For the first time in horticultural history, England led the way while Europe followed. And here our story really begins.

STOWE

LORD COBHAM'S GEORGIAN ARCADIA

Left: Built in 1741 to James Gibbs' design, the Gothic Temple was often referred to in contemporary accounts as the Gothic Church because of its ecclesiastic appearance. The pepper-pot lanterns on the lower towers and pinnacles on the main tower were added later, in an attempt to relieve the building's heaviness. Also known as the Temple of Liberty, this construction was Lord Cobham's final symbolic assault against his former Whig ally, Robert Walpole. In the confused and often contradictory symbolism of the eighteenth century, the Gothic style suggested ideals of liberty and constitutional government, which were erroneously associated with the Anglo-Saxons.

Below: This statue of King George I, depicted as the Roman emperor Marcus Aurelius, is the oldest surviving garden monument at Stowe. Originating from early on in the garden's iconography, which spans more than thirty years, it marks a time when Lord Cobham was a grateful beneficiary of the king's favour. An ardent Whig, Cobham saw the Protestant king as the defender of English liberty because the House of Hanover, to which George belonged, had wrested the throne from the Stuart dynasty, associated with the repressive forces of Catholicism and absolute monarchy.

The eighteenth century was a time of turmoil and transformation. The 1707 Act of Union had joined England and Scotland to form Great Britain. In 1714, in accordance with another parliamentary act, the Protestant Elector of Hanover became George I, establishing a foreign dynasty on the throne. The Jacobite rebellions of 1715 and 1745 attempted in vain to restore the exiled Stuart monarch, James II. Such turbulence inevitably provoked questions of identity. In addition, the financial crisis caused by the South Sea Bubble of 1720 exposed many leading politicians as corrupt; but the economy survived, spurred on by scientific advances in agriculture and the spread of industrialization. Increased wealth improved both rural and urban living conditions, leading to lower mortality rates and a surge in population. Naval dominance consolidated Britain's expanding empire, while thriving colonies in North America, India and the Caribbean contributed to its commercial power.

Horticulturally, this century saw a move away from formality. Although George London and Henry Wise continued creating grand baroque gardens into the 1730s, and neoclassical and rococo elements flourished through much of the century, the naturalistic approach rapidly gained popularity, offering a new and distinctly British landscape style. Drawing inspiration from poetry, painting, politics and patriotism, it expressed enlightenment ideas about equality and democracy, while promoting ancient rights and an ideal of natural harmony. At a time when common land was being enclosed by powerful landowners, the landscape park also provided an easy way to embellish these expanding estates, being relatively cheap to lay out and maintain. One of the earliest, most influential and glorious examples of this novel approach is the garden created over some thirty years at Stowe by Sir Richard Temple, Lord Cobham.

POWER PLAYS BETWEEN MONARCHY AND PARLIAMENT

Georgian England got off to shaky start. After the death of Queen Anne in 1714, the dull and awkward George, Elector of Hanover, as her nearest Protestant heir, grabbed the throne from the squabbling nobles and supplanted the Stuarts with the House of Hanover. While there were dozens more charismatic heirs closer in line than the Germanic George, they were all Catholic and the Act of Settlement of 1701 excluded Roman Catholics from holding the English Crown. George (right) was undermined by the Tories, who tended to uphold the divine right of kings and therefore hereditary claim of the Stuarts; he depended instead on his Whig allies, who defended the right of Parliament to determine the succession. During George I's reign, the Whigs, many of whom were ennobled by the grateful king, swept into office and stayed there for half a century – during which time they slowly shifted power from the monarchy to Parliament.

In 1715, at the age of forty, Lord Cobham married Anne Halsey, a wealthy brewer's daughter. While her pedigree added nothing to his own questionable status, her dowry enabled him to pursue his three greatest pleasures: friendship, politics and garden making. These elements came together in the family estate at Stowe, near the town of Buckingham – where Lord Cobham, a pioneer of the new style of landscape design, created what became the most famous garden in England.

Cobham's ancestors were sheep farmers who had profited richly from the rise in wool prices through the Elizabethan era. Their success was such that in around 1589 John Temple had been able to buy the manor of Stowe, thus initiating the family's vertiginous social ascent. Each of the following four generations made its mark: John's son Thomas purchased a knighthood, and then a baronetcy, from James I; his grandson Sir Peter served in Cromwell's army during the English Civil War of 1642–1649; his great-grandson, the third baronet, represented Buckingham in the House of Commons; and his great-great-grandson Richard, a distinguished soldier and devoted Whig politician, was made a baron by George I on his accession to the throne in 1714. Four years later, the king made Lord Cobham a viscount, an honour that Cobham repaid by displaying a larger-than-life statue of the king on horseback outside the North Front of his villa at Stowe.

Safely ensconced in the bosom of the Establishment, Lord Cobham set about improving his estate to create a setting that would both consolidate and proclaim his exalted status.

Below: Because of his influence as both First Lord of the Treasury and Chancellor of the Exchequer from 1721, and his leading role in the cabinet under George I and George II, Robert Walpole is regarded as Britain's first prime minister, although the term was not used at the time. Implicated in the South Sea Bubble of 1720, having sold his shares at the top of the market before the company collapsed, he survived the scandal and sheltered many of his friends from punishment, earning himself the nickname 'the skreen'. His increasing corruption and greed sparked resistance within his own Whig party and, after his unsuccessful attempts to prevent war with Spain in 1742, he was defeated in a motion of no confidence and resigned.

Above: *The Dance of the Seasons* by Claude Lorrain (c. 1602–1682) represents the cycle of life and the passing of time. Such paintings, with their Roman ruins and depictions of mortals cavorting with gods, suggest a harmony between the secular and sacred realms. Like his contemporary Nicolas Poussin, Claude Lorrain was a French artist who lived in Rome. While travelling through Europe on the Grand Tour, English aristocrats were exposed to their visions of an idealized landscape, which became the template for the gardens of classically educated landowners.

Land had long been a measure of social prestige but, as a new class of rich merchants and bankers began buying up properties from the increasingly impoverished aristocracy, it was not enough simply to have a large country estate. In that time of social ferment, taste became a measure of class – and Cobham was determined to exhibit the right kind of taste.

In this he was guided by his friends, fellow members of the Kit-Cat Club. This Whig stronghold met in a London pie house kept by Christopher (or Kit) Cat and was passionately devoted to the policies of parliamentary government, limited monarchy and Protestant succession. Its members also expressed a virulent dislike of all things French – including, in their view, vulgarity and ostentation. Among the club's more illustrious members were playwright William Congreve, architect John Vanbrugh, politician Robert Walpole, and publisher Richard Steele, who founded the *Tatler* and co-founded the *Spectator* with fellow Kit-Cat, critic Joseph Addison. While generally dismissed at the time as a witty drinking club, the Kit-Cats were later described by Walpole's son, Horace, as 'the patriots that saved Britain', because of their tireless efforts to limit the power of the monarchy while strengthening the power of parliament.

These hot-blooded young liberals expressed their reforming agenda through their plays, poetry and journalism, their art and architecture, and their dress and manners. But most notably they expressed it in their gardens and in the country estates of their friends. Deploring the autocratic formality of the previous generation, they pioneered the informal, naturalistic style which now epitomizes English garden design around the world. Not only did they bring about a revolution in style, they also established garden making as one of the great art forms. Indeed, the poet Alexander Pope declared it the noblest of arts, 'since gardening is more antique, and nearer God's own work, than poetry'.

Many theories attempt to explain the enthusiasm for this new style. It was, in part, the pendulum of fashion simply swinging from one thing to its opposite. It was also partly political: the French influence that characterized all aspects of the Stuart court seemed inappropriate for the new, relaxed

Hanoverian dynasty. The royal gardens at Versailles had marked the apogee of the formal style, perfectly expressing the tyranny of the French court in its deadening symmetry and its endless, ruler-straight avenues, perspective-defying canals, evenly spaced trees, ruthlessly clipped hedges, bland statues and ridiculous topiary. As social unrest erupted in late-seventeenth-century France, the English aristocracy was keen to distance itself from the despotism of Louis XIV. England's nobles realized they could demonstrate their own

Below: Romantic features such as this irregularly shaped pond at Stowe were considered daringly avant-garde since they represented a rejection of the formal garden. Innovative designers and garden makers opted for a looser, freer and altogether more natural approach.

enlightened philosophy through landscapes that celebrated, rather than dominated, the natural order.

There were also aesthetic reasons for the shift in style. It is impossible to ignore the influence of the Grand Tour – a sort of gap year for young aristocrats, sent off to the Continent in the company of tutors to finish their education by visiting the places they had read about in their Greek and Latin primers. While many probably spent more time exploring young flesh than old sites, they did develop a taste for classical culture, bringing back statuary, books on architecture and paintings of the Roman *campagna*, or countryside. These pictures generally depicted ancient ruins standing on sculpted hills, artfully framed by elegant trees or mirrored in meandering streams; the foregrounds were often animated by gods and peasants, pastoral sheep and sylvan deer, all bathed in the golden glow of nostalgia. Over time such images became the template for the English landscape, as young milords proclaimed themselves heirs to the republican values of Augustan Rome.

The shift towards the natural garden was to some extent driven by economic factors. Formal gardens were an extraordinarily expensive luxury. There were the initial costs of levelling land, constructing rides, walks and retaining walls, building ornamental stairs, balustrades, terraces and pavilions, and delivering a powerful enough water supply to generate fountains and irrigate earth. To all this was added the cost of plants for avenues, hedges and flower beds. Even more onerous were the costs of constant maintenance.

From the mid-seventeenth century lone voices, such as that of diplomat and essayist Sir William Temple, creator of the gardens at Moor Park, Surrey, had begun advocating a different approach. By the early eighteenth century, that whisper had become a chorus, as Whig politicians and writers joined the argument, seeing in landscape a way of promoting their new, liberal philosophy. In 1712, Joseph Addison suggested in the *Spectator* that any man 'might make a pretty landskip of his own possessions'. By taking advantage of the 'pleasant prospect' of cornfields and 'the natural embroidery of the meadows', a few carefully positioned clumps of trees could transform an estate into a garden. In 1713, Alexander Pope advised his readers in *The Guardian* to take nature as their inspiration, claiming: 'persons of genius, and those who are most capable of art, are always most fond of nature, as such are chiefly sensible, that all art consists in the imitation and study of nature.' Stephen Switzer, in his 1715 work *The Nobleman, Gentleman and Gardener's Recreation*, recommended that people tear down their walls and leave their gardens open to 'the unbounded felicities of distant prospect'. He also made the practical point that those who apply aesthetic criteria when laying out their estates – adding decorative facades to utilitarian buildings and highlighting charming views – could transform the humblest smallholding into a *ferme ornée* (ornamented farm) in which 'both profit and pleasure may be said to be agreeably mixed together'.

Nature itself, by the eighteenth century, was hardly rude and unkempt. During the century 800,000 hectares/ 2 million acres of forest and scrub were turned into cultivated farmland. Using new techniques such as crop rotation, land enclosure, drainage and afforestation, the English landscape had become a picture in itself. By the mid-century, the Scottish writer Tobias Smollett, in a letter deploring the oppression of the French tax system, extolled the English countryside as 'smiling with cultivation; the grounds exhibiting all the perfection of agriculture, parcelled out into beautiful enclosures, cornfields, hay and pasture, woodland and common'. Like their Renaissance forebears, eighteenth-century landowners opened themselves up to nature, tearing down the boundary walls and extending the garden into the

Below: Stowe was one of the first English gardens to make use of the ha-ha. This walled form of ditch, with origins that were probably French and military, came to revolutionize English garden design by blurring the distinction between man-made and natural landscapes. While protecting the grounds around the house from grazing livestock, it allowed unimpeded views across the open countryside, creating the illusion that all nature was a garden.

world beyond – and the device which enabled them to achieve this was the ha-ha.

The ha-ha was a concealed ditch surrounding the pleasure grounds: it prevented farm animals from entering while allowing those in the garden to gaze into the unobstructed park beyond. If not actually invented by John Vanbrugh (1664–1726), the device was certainly popularized by him, and it helped usher in a revolution in landscape design. Through the early years of the eighteenth century, such majestic estates as Castle Howard in North Yorkshire, Blenheim Palace in Oxfordshire and Claremont House in Surrey employed ha-has to open up grand vistas of the surrounding countryside.

It was Vanbrugh – soldier, dramatist and spy, jovial friend, generous host and self-taught architectural designer – that Lord Cobham brought in to help shape his vision for Stowe, in around 1720. From early on he also involved the landscape architect Charles Bridgeman (1690–1738). Trained at the Brompton Park Nursery in Kensington, and appointed Royal Gardener to George II in 1728, Bridgeman was schooled in the formal approach and as such might not seem the obvious choice for the forward-looking developments at Stowe. However, he was in fact one of the key figures in the transition from Anglo-Dutch formality to the freer English landscape style. While known for his parterres, avenues and geometric lakes, Bridgeman also employed such novel, natural elements as lawns, amphitheatres, wildernesses and winding paths. And he was one of the first designers to incorporate views out of the garden. While his innovations may seem tame in light of what came later, at the time they were greeted with delight by the Kit-Cats. The irascible Alexander Pope described Bridgeman as a member 'of the virtuoso class', asserting that the new garden he was creating at Stowe was a 'work to wonder at'. A generation later, Horace Walpole claimed in his *Essay on Modern Gardening* (1780) that Bridgeman's removal of enclosing walls made him one of the fathers of the new garden style. He commented: 'the capital stroke, the leading step to all that has followed was … the destruction of walls for boundaries.' The result, he continued, was that 'the garden in its turn was to be set free from its prim regularity, that it might assort with the wilder country without.'

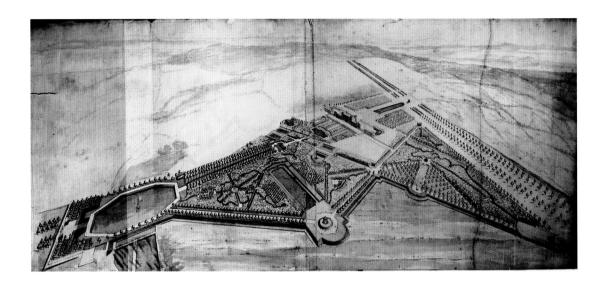

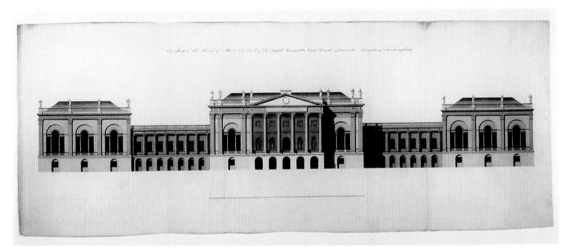

Despite the fact that no less a luminary than Sir Christopher Wren (1632–1723) had advised Cobham's father on the existing gardens and that Wren's chief joiner, William Cleare, had worked on the house, Cobham swept away all the old baroque formality. As Vanbrugh expanded the squat, domineering manor into a long, ranging Palladian villa, Bridgeman transformed the grounds. He simplified the fussy formal garden in front, added a large ornamental pool, extended the central axis down to an octagonal lake, and filled the surrounding woodlands with 'incidents' – pools, columns, an amphitheatre and an early example of a meandering path.

With no offspring of his own, Cobham gathered around him a group of young idealists whom he groomed for office; known as Cobham's Cubs, they included many of his nephews as well

Top: A plan from *Stowe Gardens in Buckinghamshire* (1739), celebrating the talents and achievements of Charles Bridgeman. Since Bridgeman had been too busy to commit his ideas to paper during his lifetime, his reputation rests largely on this book of engravings commissioned by his widow, Sarah. The most striking element in this engraving is Bridgeman's Octagonal Lake, with its central obelisk aligned on an axis with the main house.

Above: The South Front overlooking the garden was redesigned in c.1770 by the neoclassical architect Robert Adam, but his proposal did not satisfy the 2nd Earl Temple and modifications were made. Thirty-three steps were later added to descend from the central portico of the magnificent, 140 metre/ 460-foot facade to the south lawn, and the staircase parapets were topped by John Cheere's copies of the *Medici Lion*, his paw on a sphere.

Above: William Kent began life as a sign painter in Yorkshire, until his talents were recognized by a group of local gentlemen, who in 1709 sponsored him to study art in Italy. Ten years later he met Lord Burlington and returned to England, where he introduced Palladian architecture, classical mythology and naturalistic compositions to the English garden.

Right: This sculpture at Stowe is based on a life-sized Hellenistic statue, widely known as the *Medici Venus* which depicts Aphrodite, Greek goddess of love, emerging from the sea with a dolphin at her feet. A Roman version of this sculpture, of the goddess under her Roman name of Venus, featured in the Medici collection in Florence from the early seventeenth century, where it was much appreciated by young men on the Grand Tour and thus inspired further copies. These were usually in marble or bronze, whereas the Stowe Venus was gilded.

as the future prime minister, William Pitt. With Stowe now firmly entrenched at the heart of the Whig establishment, the grounds were constantly remodelled, enlarged and embellished, as a succession of the country's best designers found horticultural expressions for the Whigs' evolving ideas and achievements. In the 1730s, following the death first of Vanbrugh, then Bridgeman, their place was taken by the architect James Gibbs (1682–1754) – a rare Tory in this Whig enclave – and the designer William Kent (1685–1748). At one time an itinerant artist living in Italy, Kent had been acquired by Lord Burlington among other spoils of his Grand Tour. Having returned to England as part of Burlington's retinue, Kent proceeded to transform his patron's Chiswick House into a picturesque landscape of temples, sculptures, exedrae (semicircular structures including seats) and other Italianate features. These, although still studded with formal *patte d'oies* (paths radiating from a common point), canals and straight avenues – helped usher in the natural style.

As one of the leading lights in the new art of landscape design, it was inevitable that Kent should be soon be invited

to Stowe, where he proceeded to soften Bridgeman's layout. While he left enough formality to create an intriguing contrast, Kent changed many features to make them appear more natural. He obscured the outline of the octagonal lake to reshape it, widened paths, felled some avenues of trees, and removed boundary walls to draw in the wider landscape. As Horace Walpole later so memorably remarked: Kent 'leapt the fence, and saw that all nature was a garden'.

Kent developed Hawkwell Field as an allegorical Garden of Love – created with the help of the head gardener, appropriately named Mr Love. Amid the sweeping lawns and embosoming bowers already stood an open, domed rotunda that Vanbrugh had created in 1720, sheltering a sculpture of the goddess of love in the pose of *Venus pudica* (modest Venus, in which the naked goddess covers her breast and genitals in a gesture that draws attention to these very parts). In 1731 Kent added a more elaborate Temple of Venus, inspired by Palladian villas in the Veneto region of Italy. This temple has a central rectangular room flanked by arcades leading to two pavilions. The inscription *Veneri Hortensi* (to Venus of the Garden) carved above the main door indicates that this is a place of sexual licence; a theme reinforced by busts

of Cleopatra, Faustina, Nero and Vespasian, all famed for their sexual appetites. The interior walls depicted scenes of intrigue, and the ceiling offered an image of naked Venus to inspire those facing heavenward on couches around the room. It is hardly surprising that when the Reverend John Wesley visited in 1779 he dismissed the paintings as 'lewd'.

It was within this seductive landscape that Cobham used to entertain his friends. They gathered at the Temple of Friendship, designed by James Gibbs and decorated with allegorical images of justice, liberty and amity. This bizarre building, with its pedimented front and pyramidal roof,

BATTY LANGLEY AND THE TASTE FOR THE GOTHIC

A taste for the Gothic was promoted by the aptly named Batty Langley (1696–1751), the son of a jobbing gardener who advocated applying classical proportions to Gothic buildings. Langley was a tireless self-promoter who wrote endlessly on numerous subjects, from *An Accurate Description of Newgate* to *A Sure Method of Improving Estates*. His 1728 work *New Principles of Gardening* advocated an 'arti-natural' style, relieving the predictability of traditional formal, geometric layouts with an overlay of asymmetrical 'incidents', mazes and meandering paths. The designs he provided as illustration offer a dizzying array of writhing lines and swirling patterns. Langley was one of the influential designers who bridged the gap between formal and informal styles, although he was often ridiculed or discounted by the snobbish wits of the day. Horace Walpole claimed that all he had achieved was 'to teach carpenters to massacre that venerable species, and to give occasion to those who know nothing of the matter . . . to censure the productions of our ancestors'.

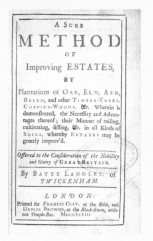

housed marble busts of Cobham and nine friends, including Frederick, Prince of Wales. Hawkwell Field also contained Gibbs' Gothic Temple. The only ironstone building in the garden, its rusty-red masonry contrasts with the smooth, creamy limestone of the other, classical buildings. A triangular construction with a tower at each of the three corners and circular rooms, it was painted inside with shields representing the ancient Anglo-Saxon kingdoms and was dedicated 'to the Liberty of our Ancestors'.

Kent's other major contribution to Stowe was the development of the Elysian Fields, a 16-hectare/40-acre wooded slope to the east of the grounds. In order to transform this rough woodland into an Arcadian valley, Cobham had to move the village of Stowe and create a new entrance to the estate. Two narrow lakes at the valley base were reconfigured as the river Styx – named after the river that in classical mythology separates the land of the living from the land of the dead. Here Kent created all manner of buildings – classical temples recalling the republican values of the Augustan age, as well as Gothic temples to evoke ancient English liberties, such as trial by jury and parliamentary representation.

While this elegiac landscape was intended to celebrate the virtuous dead of both ancient Greece and ancient Britain, what it in fact expresses is the death of Cobham's own ideals as he became increasingly disillusioned with the government of his former friend, Robert Walpole. Over the course of his decades in office it was suspected that Walpole had become ever more venal, his love of luxury expanding along with his girth. Walpole's handling of the financial crisis caused by the South Sea Bubble in 1720 appeared to protect the corrupt businessmen – himself included – who had profited by the mismanaged stock company, a joint private and public venture founded in 1711 to reduce British national debt. Even worse, however, was Walpole's controversial attempt, in 1733, to impose an excise duty on wine and tobacco. While designed to appeal to his affluent landowning supporters, this tariff would clearly punish the poor to relieve the taxes of the rich. Outraged by such an assault on civil rights and fearful of yet more taxes, Cobham joined the opposition, leading a group of discontented politicians known as the Patriot Whigs.

Right: Cobham looked to ancient Greece for the qualities he felt were missing in the politicians of his own time. The Temple of Ancient Virtue (far right), created in 1737 to a design by Kent, houses life-sized statues (right, top to bottom) of the general Epaminondas, the legendary lawmaker Lycurgus, the poet Homer and the philosopher Socrates.

Below: Designed by Kent and built in 1734, the Temple of British Worthies displays a series of busts in two distinct groups. On the left are the nation's great men of ideas, while on the right are ranged the men (and one woman) of action. In addition to the fourteen figures visible from the front of the temple, two further worthies are held in corner niches: Alexander Pope and Sir John Barnard. This temple sits across the river Styx from the Temple of Ancient Virtue.

Sir Thomas Gresham

Inigo Jones

John Milton

William Shakespeare

John Locke

Sir Isaac Newton

Sir Francis Bacon

Alfred the Great   The Black Prince   Elizabeth I   William of Orange   Sir Walter Raleigh   Sir Francis Drake   John Hampden

The excise bill ultimately failed and Walpole, humiliated, stripped Cobham of his regimental post. Cobham responded by creating a series of buildings in his Elysian Fields that promoted his own liberal values while deploring the greed and corruption of Walpole's government. In the Temple of Ancient Virtue, a peristyle rotunda inspired by the Temple of Vespa in Tivoli, were placed four life-sized statues representing the greatest general, lawmaker, poet and philosopher of ancient Greece – respectively, Epaminondas, Lycurgus, Homer and Socrates. In its shadow stood its complete opposite: the Temple of Modern Virtue, a sham ruin containing a headless bust of Robert Walpole.

Facing the Temple of Ancient Virtue across the river Styx was the Temple of British Worthies. In the centre of this stone exedra was a pyramid holding a bust of Mercury, the god who guides souls across the Styx to the underworld. Niches set into the walls of the exedra contained sixteen busts, representing great Britons lauded either for their actions or ideas. These include William Shakespeare, Sir Isaac Newton, Alfred the Great and Queen Elizabeth I; also John Hampden (one of five politicians whose attempted but unconstitutional arrest by Charles I sparked the Civil War) and Sir John Barnard, a Whig member of Parliament and opponent of Walpole. For any visitor whose grasp of history was unsure, inscriptions provided an explanation of each worthy's virtues.

With its avant-garde landscape and provocative pavilions, Stowe was soon celebrated in poetry and prose. Educated visitors would have appreciated the allegorical choices – the Path of Vice represented by the wide, easy route down to the Garden of Love, or the alternative Path of Virtue, with its steep climb up to the Elysian Fields. Classicists would have recognized in this layout the choice offered to Hercules; they might even have drawn a connection with Lord Cobham, immortalized in statue form on a column in the even more distant and inaccessible

Below: The monument to Lord Cobham, commissioned by his wife Anne and completed in 1749, the year of his death. This unusual octagonal column contains an interior staircase which spirals up 35 metres/115 feet to the viewing platform in the belvedere. From this height, visitors can see the whole of the garden laid out below. The monument could well have been inspired by the column that the Duchess of Marlborough erected in honour of her husband at Blenheim Palace in 1705.

Grecian Valley, north of the house. While today Hercules is associated with such superhuman feats as cleaning out the Augean stables, in the eighteenth century he personified piety and virtue, having attained immortality through fortitude.

Alexander Pope, a frequent visitor, names Stowe in the verse, 'Epistles to Several Persons: Epistle IV, to Richard Boyle, Earl of Burlington', first published in 1731. Essentially a treatise on taste in architecture and landscape design, Pope's poem deplores the vulgarity, vanity and expense of the formal style while, in this passage, he praises the modest, refined and elegant beauty epitomized by Lord Cobham's estate:

> . . . To build, to plant, whatever you intend,
> To rear the column, or the arch to bend,
> To swell the terrace, or to sink the grot;
> In all, let Nature never be forgot.
> But treat the Goddess like a modest fair,
> Nor overdress, nor leave her wholly bare;
> Let not each beauty ev'rywhere be spied,
> Where half the skill is decently to hide.
> He gains all points who pleasingly confounds,
> Surprises, varies, and conceals the bounds.
>
> Consult the genius of the place in all;
> That tells the waters or to rise, or fall;
> Or helps th' ambitious hill the heav'ns
>   to scale,
> Or scoops in circling theatres the vale,
> Calls in the country, catches opening glades,
> Joins willing woods, and varies shades from shades,
> Now breaks, or now directs, th' intending lines;
> Paints as you plant, and, as you work, designs.
>
> Still follow sense, of ev'ry art the soul;
> Parts answ'ring parts shall slide into a whole,
> Spontaneous beauties all around advance,
> Start ev'n from difficulty, strike from chance:
> Nature shall join you; time shall make it grow
> A work to wonder at – perhaps a Stowe . . .

Less didactic perhaps is the 'The Seasons', the major work of Scottish poet James Thomson, published in 1730. Thomson had visited the garden and celebrates Stowe's 'sheltered slopes' and 'Elysian vales' in his long passage on autumn. He exhorts:

> . . . Then lead, ye powers,
> That o'er the garden and the rural seat
> Preside, which shining through the cheerful
>   land
> In countless numbers blest Britannia sees;
> O, lead me to the wide extended walks,
> The fair majestic paradise of Stowe!

In around 1741 Cobham employed a new, young head gardener by the name of Lancelot Brown (1716–1783). There is some suggestion that Brown, born to the wife of a Northumberland farmer, may have been the illegitimate son of local barrister and member of Parliament, Sir William Loraine of Kirkharle Hall, for whom his mother had worked. One of Brown's elder brothers later married Sir William's daughter and became the steward of Kirkharle Estate, implying that the Browns were not of such humble origins as is generally assumed. Whatever his genetic heritage, Brown was clearly quick and bright. He stayed on at school until the age of sixteen – an unusually long education for a farmer's son – then went to work at Kirkharle where, over the course of the next seven years, he learnt about estate management from Sir William, who lavished much time and money on improving his lands.

Brown's move south to Buckingham, at the age of twenty-four, was perhaps provoked by the asthma which was to plague him throughout his life. Within a year he had come to the notice of Lord Cobham, who employed him as head gardener of what was, by then, the most famous garden in England. As Cobham only employed the best, Brown was privileged to be surrounded by the work of the greatest architects, engineers and designers of the day. From John Vanbrugh's pavilions he would have learnt about architecture. From Charles Bridgeman's designs he would have been confronted with the practicalities of landscaping: marking out paths, moving earth, shaping water. And from William Kent, he learnt to exploit light and shade, create balanced compositions and set buildings in the landscape.

While no particular feature at Stowe can be attributed solely to Brown, his naturalistic style infuses the whole estate.

Above: Lancelot Brown commissioned Nathaniel Dance to paint this portrait of him in around 1773. With his quiet charm and confidence, Brown rose to become the friend of peers, the prime minister, and even the king. Whereas Alexander Pope advocated consulting 'the genius of the place', Brown saw its 'capabilities', acquiring his nickname because he invariably remarked on a landscape's 'capabilities' when visiting prospective clients.

Above: The Grecian Valley. Although it appears to have been sculpted by nature over the course of millennia, this pastoral scene was created in two years by a team of men working under Lancelot Brown. They removed around 18,000 cubic metres/23,500 cubic yards of earth, using nothing more than axes, spades and wheelbarrows. While under construction, the site would have resembled a battlefield – scarred, pitted, bald and bare – but such groundwork was generally carried out in winter, while the owners were tucked away in their London residences.

It is not surprising that under Brown's stewardship a beech avenue put in place by Bridgeman to the north of the house was felled, or that the fountain-pool, parterre and basin to the south were replaced by a sweeping lawn. But the area that best exhibits Brown's style is the vast, open, grassy amphitheatre known as the Grecian Valley. In Cobham's symbolic scheme, this idyllic, naturalistic landscape represented liberty. It was inspired by James Thomson's poem 'Liberty', and its creation might well have been stimulated by the Jacobite Rising of 1745. That attempt to restore the descendants of James II to the British throne (*Jacobus* being the Latin for James) challenged parliamentary authority by ignoring the Act of Settlement, and thus threatened the liberties that the ageing Lord Cobham held so dear.

In the valley stood the eponymous Grecian Temple: this was the sort of garden construction that Brown would later eschew in his own designs, even if favoured by his classically educated patrons. He preferred to focus on nature itself. Raising a hillside, lowering a valley, sculpting a slope to balance or enhance a view, removing a wood, adjusting the course of a river – this was his domain. The essential elements were a lake to reflect the villa at the heart of the composition, the

PLATE IV.

VIEW of the MACHINE in MOTION, and of
A TREE DURING TRANSPORTATION.

Left: Lancelot Brown took the informal landscape park and stripped it back to its basic elements: an enclosing belt of trees, a reflecting lake, a smooth, plinth-like lawn. This view towards the South Front of the villa would have looked very different before Brown's arrival at Stowe in 1741, when it still bore the imprint of Bridgeman's formal design. Above: An illustration of Brown's ingenious invention for moving trees, from *The Planter's Guide* (1827) by Henry Steuart. As much an engineer as he was a garden designer, Brown developed this machine so he could transport mature trees more easily. Replanted in the landscape, they provided the instant air of age that was necessary if his patrons were to enjoy his designs within their lifetime.

whole placed in a smooth meadow, framed by delicate groves and enclosed by a belt of trees. In short, Brown perfected the work of God to create a calm, harmonious, natural scene.

Not averse to devising an occasional temple or ruin, Brown even designed the Palladian villas at Croome Court in Worcestershire, and Claremont in Surrey. But his instinct was to remove from the garden all buildings, sculptures, monuments and ruins; and with them, any arcane references and outmoded allusions. Towards the end of the century many lead statues, rendered unfashionable by his austere vision, were melted down for bullets and sent off to America, where they came to be used in the War of Independence of 1775–1783. Brown was also quick to move utilitarian eyesores such as kitchen gardens, stables and sheds. Indeed, whole villages were eliminated if they could not be screened.

Inevitably, Brown's work was noticed with envy by Lord Cobham's neighbours and political friends. Cobham was generous with his head gardener's time and soon Brown was advising landowners up and down the country on how to improve the natural look of their estates. Efficient and competent, Brown was good at interpreting his clients' wishes and showed a regard for their finances. He was often required to move large trees to create a look of maturity; this was a risky process and one that many trees did not survive. Others before him, including the diarist John Evelyn, had invented machines for transporting live trees, but Brown's method was easier (even if losses were still high). It involved laying the tree horizontally rather than keeping it vertical. Roots would be cut and a pole, fitted with wheels at one end, would be lashed to the tree before it was levered out into a horizontal position, root ball attached. A team of strong horses would then pull the contraption to the desired destination.

Over the course of his career Brown created, designed, advised on, or inspired hundreds of landscapes throughout England and 'immortal Brown' is credited with reshaping not only the English landscape, but the English idea of landscape.

By 1744 Stowe was so popular that Benton Seeley, a local writing master, created a guide to the estate: *A Description of the Gardens of Lord Viscount Cobham, at Stow in Buckinghamshire* is believed to be the first garden guide ever published. It was so successful that it was reprinted seventeen times before the end of the century, and it launched Seeley's career as a printer and publisher. While his guide was a major force in promoting Stowe's reputation, it also influenced the fashion for garden visiting. As soldiers and politicians – such as Lord Carlisle at Castle Howard, General Dormer at Rousham, or the Duke of Marlborough at Blenheim – retired to cultivate their gardens, poets and journalists commented on their efforts. Gardening was part of the national conversation.

The general public, taking advantage of improvements in both roads and carriages, flocked to see what the fuss was about. Before long, other enterprising publishers were producing guides to the important gardens of the day. Visitors could purchase these from local inns, many of which sprang up primarily to serve the garden-visiting public. Describing the art and furnishings of the house in addition to buildings and statuary in the grounds, such guides often provided itineraries so that eager visitors could make the most of their limited time. Other, more enterprising visitors would simply ask the housekeeper or head gardener to give them a tour in exchange for a small tip. Such gratuities provided a welcome supplement to modest salaries; Horace Walpole bitterly remarked that to help cover the cost of building works at Strawberry Hill, his Gothic castle in Twickenham, he should have married his housekeeper – she had grown rich by showing visitors around.

Right and following pages: Over the course of the eighteenth century, Stowe evolved from a typical baroque garden into a pioneering English landscape park. Under its three main designers, Bridgeman (who was involved c.1711-1735), Kent (1730-1748) and Brown (1741-1751), the garden grew increasingly naturalistic. Eradicating the formal geometry of the previous age, Stowe's meandering streams, rolling lawns and freely growing trees represented liberty in Lord Cobham's elaborate allegorical programme. They also ushered in a radically new, natural style of landscape design. Cobham's heir, Richard, the 2nd Earl Temple, continued the naturalizing process while adding neoclassical facades to several of the temples. The overall landscape did not evolve much under Richard's successors, although they added minor features in keeping with the tastes of the times.

Left and below: James Gibbs' Palladian Bridge of 1738 was inspired by a similar bridge at Wilton House, Wiltshire, but is set lower into the ground and incorporates ramps instead of steps. This is because it was designed for horse-drawn carriages rather than for foot passage. It originally crossed the stream that emptied into the Octagonal Lake, but now sits in the woods at the eastern end of the garden.

Within decades Stowe's reputation had spread not only across the Channel, but across the Russian steppes and the Atlantic Ocean as well. The French came in such numbers that *Les Charmes de Stow*, a guide in French, was published in 1748. Several years later, the philosopher Jean-Jacques Rousseau visited and described Stowe as a series of beautiful, natural scenes, adding: 'the master and creator of this superb domain has also erected ruins, temples and ancient buildings, which, like the scenes, exhibit a magnificence which is more than human.' When Catherine the Great commissioned Wedgwood to create the 'Frog Service' for her summer palace in 1773, it was decorated with scenes of British gardens – and Stowe's fame was such that it apparently featured in 48 of the 952 images. From America, John Adams and Thomas Jefferson, both future presidents of the United States, visited together in 1786; while Jefferson conceded that the estate was 'superb', the dispossession of small independent farmers through land enclosure offended his agrarian ideals.

Indeed, Brown's 'improvement' of the English landscape was not universally applauded. The social changes it reflected caused great consternation to the more conscientious members

Below: Brown's work appeals to the modern, minimalist sensibility, but there were many in his time who were horrified by the destructive consequences of the landscape park: the loss of many great formal gardens, along with the busy patchwork of countryside that once surrounded them.

of the thinking public. By banishing villages to enhance the view, it was feared that the easy relationship between landlord and tenant was being severed. By replacing the busy patchwork of livestock, crops, woodland and villages with Brown's smooth, empty landscapes, it appeared that the diversity of agricultural produce was reduced to a monoculture. Oliver Goldsmith's poem 'The Deserted Village', published in 1770, expresses his abhorrence at the rural depopulation being caused by those in the pursuit of the landscape style. Lord Cobham appears to exemplify Goldsmith's immoral 'man of wealth and pride', who:

> . . . Takes up a space that many poor supplied;
> Space for his lake, his park's extended bounds,
> Space for his horses, equipage, and hounds;
> The robe that wraps his limbs in silken sloth,
> Has robbed the neighbouring fields of half
> their growth;

SPORTING LIFE

Despite the novel aesthetics and arcane allusions of the eighteenth-century landscape park, it must not be forgotten that these estates were at the same time commercial enterprises. The woods provided timber and the lawns were grazed by livestock. They were also landscapes of pleasure, and, as hunting was still the favourite sport, all elements were turned to that end. Woodland was needed to feed and house deer, shrubberies for birds, lakes for fishing, open fields were necessary for coursing hare (in which dogs attempt to outrun their prey and turn their course rather than capture them, a sport that in its decline gave rise to dog racing). Long, serpentine carriage drives were necessary to lead the ladies around in an elegant fashion, while straight gallops allowed the gentlemen to exercise their mounts.

His seat, where solitary sports are seen,
Indignant spurns the cottage from the green . . .

Many later blamed Brown for shifting social as well as aesthetic attitudes, although it could be said that he simply reflected the spirit of the times. The enclosure of common ground had begun in the Middle Ages, but the process was greatly accelerated in the eighteenth century. Many millions of acres were taken into private ownership as canny landowners, making use of advances in science, set out fully to exploit the land's potential for profit. Seen in this context, Brown's effect on the landscape is not so grave.

For nearly a century after Cobham's death in 1749, Stowe remained closely associated with the vibrant and often tumultuous political life of the nation. King George II had made Cobham's sister Countess Temple in her own right so that her son, Richard Grenville-Temple (1711–1779), heir to the estate, could become the 2nd Earl Temple. He was well connected to the centre of power: both his brother, George Grenville, and brother-in-law William Pitt, served as prime minister. Stowe passed next to Richard's nephew, the statesman George Nugent-Temple-Grenville (1753–1813), who served as Lord Lieutenant of Ireland and, in 1784, was made Marquess of Buckingham by King George III. The Marquess was succeeded by his son Richard (1776–1839), who held various ministerial offices, but broke with family tradition by becoming a Tory. His support for Lord Liverpool's government was rewarded in 1822 – and the family's rise through the peerage – when King George IV made him Duke of Buckingham and Chandos.

Stowe's successive heirs, whose wealth increased through advantageous marriages, made various changes to the gardens over this period – but none matched Lord Cobham for passion, vision and drive. Although William Kent had died in 1748 and Lancelot Brown moved on to London to establish his own landscape practice two years later, Cobham's nephew, Richard Grenville-Temple, continued to develop the landscape park with the help of his own gardener, Richard Woodward. He also altered the Grecian Temple, resuming the allegorical discourse begun by his uncle by renaming it the Temple of Concord and Victory. He inscribed the words

Above: This 30-metre/100-foot obelisk was originally designed by Vanbrugh to sit in the centre of the Octagonal Lake. In keeping with a continued programme of naturalizing the grounds after Lord Cobham's death, his nephew and successor Richard moved the obelisk to the north-west corner of the garden. He dedicated it to General Wolfe, whose victory in the battle for Quebec in 1759 cost him his life, but secured Canada for the British.

Left: This grotto-like exedra, designed by Kent in around 1739, provided a sheltered alcove in which to sit and view the park. It was ornamented with coloured pebbles spelling out the family motto, later punningly adopted by the 2nd Earl Temple: *Templa quam dilecta* – How lovely are thy temples. The motto echoes a biblical phrase and pays tribute to what Lord Cobham so exuberantly expressed in three dimensions throughout his landscape.

'*Concordiae et victoriae*' on the entablature and dedicated it to Britain's triumph in the Seven Years' War. He also erected an obelisk to commemorate General Wolfe's 1759 victory over the French at Quebec – a feat which cost the general his life, but secured Canada as a British colony. Several temples were demolished in the next generation by George, Marquess of Buckingham, whose addition of a menagerie surrounded by formal flower gardens reflected the new trend for greater drama in the garden. His son, Richard, the 1st Duke, purchased Lamport Field to the east and, with his head gardener James Brown, expanded the garden yet further.

From the mid-nineteenth century, Stowe's fortunes began a decline that was almost as dramatic as its ascent had been 300 years before. In 1839 the estate was inherited by Richard, the arrogant and profligate 2nd Duke of Buckingham and Chandos (1797–1861). Robert Peel made him a Privy Councillor, then Lord Keeper of the Privy Seal – one of the highest offices of state. Remarkably, given his position in society and the enormous wealth he inherited, the 2nd Duke managed to run up debts of over a million pounds. This did not prevent him from lobbying the prime minister to secure a royal visit in 1845, nor from

Below: Dating from 1738, this delicate pavilion made of wood and painted canvas was one of the first chinoiserie buildings to appear in an English garden. Originally placed on stilts in a pond near the Elysian Fields, it was moved in around 1750, having been deemed inappropriate to an Arcadian scene. The building was later sold, but the National Trust managed to purchase it back in 1993 and restored it to its present glory. It now sits in the Japanese Garden, which features water gardens and rockeries created in the early nineteenth century by the decadent 2nd Duke of Buckingham and Chandos. The influential garden writer John Claudius Loudon, visiting in 1831, noted approvingly: 'nature has done little or nothing; man a great deal, and time has improved his labours.'

Above: Queen Victoria arriving at the North Front in January 1845, as featured in *The Illustrated London News*. Unfortunately, this prestigious event in Stowe's history also contributed to its downfall. Lavish preparations for the queen's three-day visit sunk the family deeper in debt, with the result that they were forced to auction off the contents of the house a few years later.

lavishing expense on entertaining Queen Victoria and Prince Albert. The puritanical monarch was not impressed with his hospitality, and the three-day event left the duke deeper in debt. Industrious Victorians had little sympathy for the foibles of the rich: in 1847, the duke was forced to flee the country to escape creditors who, in an earlier age, might respectfully have turned a blind eye. The family was declared bankrupt. Forced to sell the contents of the house, in 1848 they held an auction on the estate which lasted a full forty days. Centuries of carefully accumulated property, furniture, art and even alcohol – 21,000 bottles of wine and 500 bottles of spirits – were auctioned off. Mature trees were felled and sold, along with garden sculptures. In total 14,500 hectares/35,800 acres of ancestral land was sold, reducing the estate to 4,000 hectares/10,000 acres. The duke brought further social opprobrium on the family by seeking a divorce at a time when to do so required an act of parliament.

During the remainder of the nineteenth century, the grounds at Stowe succumbed to neglect. With the garden staff reduced from forty to four, temples disintegrated, lakes silted up, the ha-ha collapsed and paths disappeared beneath undergrowth. In 1921, the Reverend Luis Morgan-Grenville, Stowe's childless heir, sold the house, gardens and part of the park to pay off the debts that continued to plague his family. The following year the estate was bought by the governors of Stowe School. One of the few changes they made was to replace a Temple of Bacchus with a chapel designed by the Scottish architect Robert Lorimer – clearly a better example for pubescent school boys. In 1989, the estate received an endowment which enabled the National Trust to take on the gardens and begin a long, expensive restoration. In 1997 the house, now Grade I listed, was also taken into the ownership of the Stowe House Preservation Trust, although it continues to serve as a school.

Above: The Queen's Temple in a near-derelict state, captured in a photograph taken some years after the sale of Stowe in 1921. The temple was restored by the National Trust in the 1990s.
Right: Originally named the Lady's Temple, this structure was designed by Gibbs in 1742 as a place where Lady Cobham could entertain friends. It was remodelled in the late-eighteenth century to give it a neoclassical air, and renamed the Queen's Temple in 1790 to commemorate Queen Charlotte's role in helping George III recover from madness.

Eighteenth-century naturalism had been ushered in by an advocate of the oriental style, Sir William Temple. In an odd parallel, its demise was sounded a century later by another orientalist, Sir William Chambers. Temple's *Upon the Gardens of Epicurus* (1685) had proposed an informal, asymmetrical, natural approach; conversely, Chambers' *Dissertation on Oriental Gardening* (1772) argued for more variety and incident in the landscape. Chambers' work was a veiled attack on the ubiquity of Brown's sweeping, monumental style. In it, he deplored 'an indiscriminate application of the same manner, upon all occasions, however opposite, or ill adapted'. Unlike Temple, who had derived his ideas from imported Chinese art, Chambers had actually visited China. His fascination with oriental architecture culminated in the 1757 publication *Designs of Chinese Buildings*, which inspired Augusta, the Dowager Princess of Wales, to commission him to design her garden at Kew. Chambers designed more than twenty-five buildings for Kew, the most famous is probably the ten-storey Pagoda, whose instant popularity reflects a general shift from the naturalism which had dominated garden making for the previous two generations, to something less predictable and more visually exciting.

ROUSHAM HOUSE

Just as Versailles had embodied the absolute monarchy of the French court, Stowe expressed the liberal philosophy of the Whigs. However, it was not long before other landowners, regardless of their politics, were also embracing the landscape style. When Kent first arrived at Stowe, he had already begun creating his glorious gardens at Rousham, Oxfordshire, for General James Dormer, who had been wounded in the Battle of Blenheim. Essentially a meditation on sex and death, Rousham combined the formal with the natural, the military with the Arcadian.

On the upper terrace, a Jacobean manor sits on a smooth, bowling-green lawn, backed by Peter Scheemakers' sculpture of a lion mauling a horse. The lawn is flanked by stone pillars, or herms, topped with carved heads of Minerva, goddess of war, while a sculpture of the 'The Dying Gaul', also by Scheemakers, languishes nearby. A meandering path leaves this melancholy martial space to descend through scented woodland, where roses, lilacs and honeysuckle embellish the darker laurels and conifers. Below, an open meadow is filled with joyful evocations of the pagan age: a handsome statue of Antinous stares out across the river, while a leering Pan and satyr spy on a naked Venus. As at Stowe, this Arcadian valley is filled with classical temples, Gothic facades and busts of inspiring characters from ancient myths and British history, reprising that favoured combination of English liberties and Republican values. The path meanders on to end in a glorious walled garden, an earthly paradise after the cares of the mortal world and fantasies of the classical past.

STOURHEAD

Another much-loved eighteenth-century landscape park is Stourhead, in Wiltshire. Having steered the family bank through the South Sea Bubble, Henry Hoare profited handsomely enough from the crisis to develop the vast estate, purchased in 1717. His son, Henry Hoare II, dammed a string of fish ponds in the valley to make a dramatic three-pronged lake, then proceeded to reshape and plant up the steep surrounding slopes. Eschewing the services of professional designers, this talented amateur created a

Above: This statue formed part of the Arcadian landscape that William Kent created at Rousham between 1737 and 1741, over Bridgeman's earlier, more formal design. Inspired by a classical sculpture dating from the third century BC and representing the triumph of Tivoli over Rome, Peter Scheemakers' poignant image of a lion attacking a horse also suggests the triumph of savagery over civilization. It is sited at the point where Rousham's wilderness meets the formal landscape.

Above: Henry Hoare designed the garden at Stourhead as an allegorical depiction of the journey of Aeneas, Trojan prince and legendary founder of Rome. Monuments and temples subtly drew the visitor through the garden, where plantings were designed to evoke different moods. In classic eighteenth-century style, the garden was created around an artificial lake, formed by damming a stream on the valley floor.

lakeside circuit studded with a series of tableaux recalling Aeneas's journey into the underworld, and his subsequent ascent towards enlightenment and the founding of the new empire of Rome. The landscape, which Horace Walpole described as 'one of the most picturesque scenes in the world', reflects the influence of the French seventeenth-century landscape paintings which Hoare acquired on his Grand Tour. Indeed, certain scenes appear to be copied directly from Hoare's own painting of Claude Lorrain's *Landscape with Aeneas at Delos*. The allegorical programme, conveyed through temples, grotto, sculptures and ruins is somewhat obscured by later Gothic additions – a King Alfred's Tower, rustic Watch Cottage and Hermitage. Over-enthusiastic planting in the nineteenth century, especially of invasive *Rhododendron ponticum*, undermined the smooth clarity of the original landscape, but much of this has been removed and the original planting restored.

STUDLEY ROYAL AND RUINS OF FOUNTAINS ABBEY

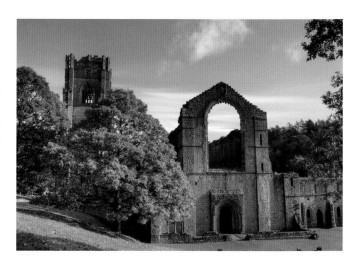

John Aislabie's fortunes emerged relatively unscathed from the South Sea Bubble scandal. An ambitious Tory member of Parliament, he had risen in 1718 to become Chancellor of the Exchequer, in which capacity he promoted the South Sea project. When the scheme collapsed, Aislabie was accused of corruption, expelled from Parliament and banned from public office for life. Retreating to the family estate of Studley Royal in North Yorkshire, Aislabie set about creating a water garden in the dramatic wooded valley. Here, a still, formal water parterre, canals, pool and crescent ponds are set in smooth green lawns studded with statuary. Later, in what seems like a declaration of repentance, he created a classical Temple of Piety on a mound reflected in the pool. Throughout his life, Aislabie tried to buy the neighbouring ruin of Fountains Abbey, a magnificent Cistercian building that had been destroyed in Henry VIII's dissolution of the monasteries. But it was not until 1767, after Aislabie's death, that his son William finally managed to purchase the ruins. William extended the gardens to incorporate this picturesque feature, softening the grand, rectilinear austerity of his father's design to create a more curvaceous landscape in the romantic style then coming into fashion.

Above: The ruins of Fountains Abbey, founded by Cistercians in the twelfth century, were coveted by John Aislabie, owner of neighbouring Studley Royal. Unable to acquire the abbey for himself, Aislabie instead created a vast water garden that climaxes in a woodland view of the dramatic ruins. After Aislabie's death, his son finally purchased Fountains Abbey and incorporated it into the estate, transforming the formal water garden into a romantic woodland landscape.

WEST WYCOMBE PARK

Benjamin Franklin, one of America's founding fathers, described West Wycombe as 'a paradise'. But this famous landscape garden in Buckinghamshire has none of the piety of Stowe, the erudition of Stourhead, or the repentance of Studley Royal – and it certainly has none of Rousham's bittersweet serenity. West Wycombe was designed as a pleasure ground for the notorious libertine, Sir Francis Dashwood. It demonstrates the shift from Lancelot 'Capability' Brown's idealized naturalism to a more picturesque style, full of incident and exotica. Inspired by his youthful Grand Tour of Italy – during which time, Horace Walpole claimed, he was seldom sober – Dashwood returned home and created a Palladian villa set in an elegant garden of woodlands, meadows and carefully contrived vistas. The grounds were sprinkled with delights – a rockwork cascade presided over by two water nymphs, an oriental tent, monuments, mausolea and memorials – all rather

Below: West Wycombe, the most theatrical, and most Italianate, of English eighteenth-century gardens. It was laid out in the conventional style of the time as a walk around a central lake, its wooded slopes sprinkled with pavilions inspired by classical Greek and Italian originals. The Temple of Music (below), which was used as a theatre, is based on Rome's Temple of Vesta. The Temple of Flora, a summerhouse, resembles a small temple on Athens' Acropolis. An octagonal tower was inspired by the Tower of the Four Winds, also in Athens, while cockfights were held in the Roman-style triumphal arch.

tongue-in-cheek. One of the most intriguing installations were the Hellfire Caves. Winding over 800 metres/half a mile into the hillside, they boasted various chambers for nefarious purposes, a banqueting hall, and an inner temple that sits 90 metres/300 feet beneath the local church and can only be accessed by crossing the mythical river Styx. In the fashion of the day, Dashwood flooded the valley floor to create a 3.6-hectare/9-acre lake; but his lake, unusually, was swan-shaped and fitted with a Spanish galleon. On one of the lake's three islands, he placed the classical Temple of Music, which presents a pretty view from the house. The temple served as a discreet and inaccessible rendezvous for private encounters, while doubling up as a theatre for Dashwood's more public entertainments. A founder member of the Society of Dilettanti – a group of wealthy gentlemen whose aim was to promote classical taste in England – Dashwood was better-known for the Hellfire Club, which he also founded. It was a drinking club which promoted free love and provoked scandal among the gentle-folk of the nearby village.

BIDDULPH GRANGE

BIDDULPH GRANGE

JAMES BATEMAN'S VICTORIAN WORLD GARDEN

James Bateman was extremely fortunate in several particulars: he was born into a wealthy family, he met a woman who shared his passion for plants, and he befriended an artist who gave form to his wildest horticultural fantasies. Together the three of them, James Bateman, his wife Maria Sybilla Egerton-Warburton and their friend Edward Cooke, created one of the most intriguing, bizarre and memorable gardens of the Victorian era. While eighteenth-century horticulture had been shaped by poets and philosophers, in the nineteenth century the mantle shifted to merchants and industrialists. Where the eighteenth-century garden had been a place of ideas and allusions, the nineteenth-century garden was a didactic space. Unencumbered by the classical education and the liberal – if not libertarian – values of their horticultural forebears, this new generation of garden makers was interested in technology, science and natural history. Victorian gardens were a celebration of Empire, a catalogue of nature, a collection of exotica; they reflected the adventurous, international spirit of the age. And nowhere is this spirit more exuberantly expressed than in Bateman's garden at Biddulph Grange.

James Bateman (1811–1897) was the only child of an affluent industrialist. His grandfather, an unscrupulous but extremely successful Lancashire entrepreneur, made a fortune in collieries, ironworks and cotton mills. He purchased the neighbouring estates of Knypersley Hall and Biddulph Grange in the industrial heartland of Staffordshire, intending to exploit their abundant coal reserves. Meanwhile his son, John Bateman, moved into Knypersley Hall soon after the birth of his only child

Below: James Bateman inherited enormous wealth from coal and engineering. Eschewing the industry of his forefathers, he studied botany and became an internationally respected orchidologist before bankrupting himself by creating a grand garden. Right: With Italian and American gardens, Scottish glen, Himalayan slopes, Egyptian tomb and Chinese temple, Biddulph expressed what Geoffrey Jellicoe described as 'a new era of British Internationalism'.

and proceeded to improve the property in the fashion of the time. As the estate had not yet been absorbed into the expanding suburbs, nor had it been blighted by the industrial activity of the nearby foundries, John Bateman developed parkland, commissioning a picturesque Gothic tower to overlook Knypersley Pool – a large reservoir that had been dug on the edge of the estate in the 1820s as a feeder for the Trent and Mersey Canal. In the valley below was the ancient Gawton Well, the waters of which were said to have curative powers, and nearby was a dolmen that many believed was used by druids as a sacrificial altar. It was in this romantic landscape that the young James Bateman explored nature and discovered, at his mother's knee, an early love of flowers.

Above: The Spode plate, commissioned to celebrate James Bateman's twenty-first birthday, shows Knypersley Hall framed by local features, probably drawn by Bateman himself.
Below: Named after the twelfth-century Arabic philosopher Averroës, *Averrhoa carambola* is an exotic tree more commonly known today as the star fruit. Bateman's prowess at fruiting it probably owed something to Knypersley's head gardener, Patrick Don, whose father became curator of the Royal Botanic Garden, Edinburgh.

Clearly a precocious and much-indulged child, Bateman developed a passion for rare plants while at Oxford. His earliest interest was in tropical fruit and, in 1833 while still an undergraduate at Magdalen College, he gave his first talk at the august Royal Horticultural Society, presenting a paper on *Averrhoa carambola*. Having purchased a specimen of this pretty, little evergreen tree the previous year from a Hammersmith nursery, Bateman had managed to coax it to fruit in one of Knypersley's many greenhouses. This was the first time an *Averrhoa carambola* was fruited in England and it was quite a coup for the novice botanist.

But it was a casual visit to Thomas Fairburn's nursery, on the site of modern-day Keble College, Oxford, which really shifted Bateman's focus and shaped his future. Fairburn showed the young scholar a cutting of *Renanthera coccinea*, a tropical Asian orchid that attaches to rocks by its aerial roots. As Bateman later explained, 'this sealed my fate' and orchids became 'the master passion' of his life. Turning his back on the industry that had fuelled his family's fortunes, Bateman decided to dedicate himself to plants, and he did so with all the ruthless zeal that his ancestors had applied to the making of money.

Trawling through London nurseries, Bateman began to build up a collection of orchids. One of his main suppliers was James Veitch & Sons

Below: Having purchased his first *Renanthera coccinea* for a guinea, Bateman spent the rest of his life studying orchids. The English botanist John Lindley introduced the word 'orchid' as an anglicized form of *Orchis* – a scientific name derived from the ancient Greek word for testicle, in reference to the shape of certain orchid root tubers. In Greek mythology Orchis, the son of a nymph and a satyr, became inebriated at a Bacchic festival and attempted to rape a priestess. He was duly torn apart by the outraged revellers and, when his father begged the gods to restore Orchis to life, they transformed him into a flower whose form recalls the danger of unbridled lust.

in the King's Road, but there were many other sources, including Henderson's in Paddington, Hugh Low's in Clapton and Stevens' in Covent Garden, where many rare plants were auctioned; not to mention foreign suppliers such as M. Fromane of Toulouse and Linden in Belgium. Bateman soon established a lively correspondence with many experts in the field, including the Director of the Royal Botanic Gardens at Kew, Dr Joseph Hooker.

It was in 1833 that Bateman commissioned his first plant-hunting trip, sponsoring Fairburn's foreman, Thomas Colley, to travel to British Guiana in search of orchids. Although the trip was not particularly successful it gave Bateman a taste for the chase. Of the sixty different kinds of orchid Colley sent back, about a third of them were new to science, though not particularly remarkable. In 1834 the botanist John Lindley (1799–1865) named one of Colley's new specimens *Batemannia colleyi* to commemorate the expedition.

Among the few treasures Colley did secure was *Oncidium lanceanum*, a species named after the barrister, J.H. Lance, who first discovered it on a tamarind tree near Government House in Surinam several years earlier. The orchid's appearance in London had caused such a stir that Lance was awarded a Silver Medal by the Royal Horticultural Society. So Colley, recognizing the value of the species when he found it during the expedition, and aware that another professional collector was working nearby, stripped the tree of every single specimen. Such cut-throat tactics were common among plant hunters. While some would spread misinformation about locations to deter rivals, others would destroy any specimens that they could not carry to prevent competitors from acquiring the same material, or even fell whole forests simply to harvest the few high-growing orchids. In 1835 Bateman wrote an account of Colley's expedition for John Claudius Loudon's *Gardener's Magazine*; his comment that 'nor, so far as I know, has the species ever been found before or since in that country' suggests a self-satisfied delight in response to the act of vandalism carried out by his plant hunter.

In the early nineteenth century orchids were a great status symbol. Wealthy collectors were prepared to pay a

Right: The orchid *Batemannia colleyi* was named by John Lindley to commemorate the first plant-hunting expedition sponsored by Bateman. Today some species are extremely valuable and orchid smuggling is rife, despite the ban on collecting orchids in the wild that was put in place by the 1973 Convention on International Trade in Endangered Species (CITES).

high price to acquire them, though not as high as many plant hunters paid to secure them. Plant hunting was a hazardous business and intrepid adventurers risked their lives to satisfy the lust for orchids and other unusual foreign plants which gripped the horticultural community. Tropical diseases, wild animals, poisonous insects, extremes of heat and cold, floods, frosts, angry locals and cut-throat competitors were just a few of the dangers they faced. In the eighteenth century Jesuit priests had been among the first to send back specimens, seeds, cultivation details and images of new plants. By the nineteenth century plant hunting was big business, with individual collectors and commercial nurseries financing expeditions lasting up to two years.

One of the greatest collectors ever, David Douglas (1798–1834), allegedly fell into a pit trap in Hawaii and, unable to escape, was gored to death by a bull. In the early twentieth century, the French missionary and botanist Jean-André Soulié (1858–1905) was tortured and shot by Tibetan monks enraged at the recent British invasion, in which hundreds of Tibetan peasants had been massacred. George Forrest (1873–1932) and Reginald Farrer (1880–1920) both died in the field, Forrest of a heart attack while in Yunnan and Farrer in Burma, probably of alcohol poisoning. Rather more successful was Frank Kingdon-Ward (1885–1958) who lived to a reasonable age, even though in his fifty-year plant-hunting career he experienced being impaled on a bamboo spike, falling off a cliff, being lost for days without food and having his tent crushed by falling trees. Ernest 'Chinese' Wilson (1876–1930) had his leg smashed in an avalanche of rocks while on a lily-hunting expedition, leaving him with a permanent 'lily-limp'. Having begun his career hunting Chinese plants for James Veitch & Sons, Wilson ultimately introduced about 1,000 Asian species to the West, sixty of which now bear his name.

Though orchidomania reached its height in the early Victorian period, orchids had been imported into England for centuries. As early as 1640 John Parkinson recorded the arrival of an American slipper orchid; in the 1770s Sir Joseph Banks was collecting orchids in Australia and towards the end of the century, ships' captains like William Bligh were bringing orchids and other plant bounty back to Kew. But in those early years few understood the needs of the plants and survival

Above: Though he started as a gardener's boy at Scone Palace in Scotland, David Douglas became one of the world's greatest plant collectors. In 1823 he went to the east coast of North America and collected fruit trees and oaks. A year later he went to America's west coast, sending back seeds and nearly 500 plants. Among his introductions was the Douglas fir, *Pseudotsuga menziesii*.
Below: Captain William Bligh ferried orchids across the sea to the Royal Botanic Gardens at Kew.
Below right: The Theresia Estate tea plantation in Ceylon in the 1800s.

THE WARDIAN CASE: A PASSPORT FOR PLANTS

In the early nineteenth century the physician Dr Nathaniel Bagshaw Ward noticed that a few fern spores, which had been inadvertently sealed in a bottle, had germinated and were growing well. Anxious to protect his precious ferns from London's polluted air, he built a glass box – an early terrarium – and found that his ferns flourished in the enclosed microclimate. Realizing the wider implications of his invention, in 1833 he created large glazed cases and successfully transported live plants to Australia. By preventing damage from salty sea air, lack of fresh water, exposure and neglect, the Wardian case enabled live plants to survive on deck for months at a time, allowing the large-scale transportation of plants from the farthest corners of the globe and opening the way for international commercial exploitation of plants. It was in Wardian cases that Robert Fortune secreted 20,000 tea plants out of China and shipped them to India to establish tea plantations in the British colony. Similarly, rubber-tree seedlings were shipped from Brazil to Kew in Wardian cases; having been grown on they were then shipped off to Malaya (in current-day Malaysia) to start that country's lucrative rubber industry.

rates were low, with as many as half of each shipment dying in transit. In 1818 the ornithologist William John Swainson is said to have packed a box of plants for shipping from Rio de Janeiro using dormant orchids – which he mistook for weeds – as insulation. When the shipment arrived in London the orchids were in full blossom, delighting the public and sparking a wave of orchid fever similar to the tulipomania that swept Holland in the seventeenth century. While this story has been called into question (it being unlikely that such an experienced naturalist could be unaware of the material he was using), certainly by the 1820s orchidomania was in full swing. New introductions were often sold at auction and commanded enormous prices. Soon amateurs and professional nurserymen were attempting to cultivate their own orchids. As they experimented with propagation techniques and learned more about the plants' natural habitats they became more successful. In 1852 Benjamin S. Williams published the first edition of *The Orchid-Grower's Manual*, bringing the hobby within the reach of more modest fanciers.

Bateman derived great kudos from his *Oncidium lanceanum*, noting how, when word got out that he possessed plants of this rare species, people would 'go down on their knees … offering their greatest treasures in exchange'. This prestige was clearly one of the appeals of orchid growing for Bateman. Buoyed by his early success, at the age of twenty-six he set out to consolidate his reputation by writing a monograph on orchids. Published in ten volumes from 1837 to 1843, it was the largest botanical work ever produced, an elephant folio entitled *Orchidaceae of Mexico and Guatemala*. Bateman's major source of plant material was George Ure Skinner, a British merchant working in Guatemala. On discovering that Skinner had provided bird specimens to Manchester's Museum of Natural History, Bateman contacted Skinner and urged him to send orchids to Knypersley. Bateman also visited the major collections in Europe and England – a task that gained him entrée to such noble persons as the Duke of Devonshire and the 6th Earl of Stamford, along with the more lowly scholars and clerics who made up the bulk of Victorian orchid fanciers.

Bateman's *Orchidaceae* describes each orchid in Latin and English, provides its habitat, details its discovery and recounts its introduction to Europe. The book was lavishly illustrated with exquisitely hand-coloured lithographic plates, most of which were prepared by Augusta Withers and

Right: This hand-coloured lithographic plate appears in James Bateman's giant book entitled *Orchidaceae of Mexico and Guatemala*, which he dedicated to Queen Adelaide. Bateman corresponded with many experts in the field, and through the publication of this monograph in Latin and English confirmed his own standing as a botanist.

CATASETUM MACULATUM.

Pub.d by J. Ridgway & Sons, 169 Piccadilly, July 1st, 1837.

Sarah Anne Drake. Only 125 copies of the *Orchidaceae* were printed and few of those sold, though the list of subscribers indicates that Bateman's orchids had introduced him to an agreeably elite and international coterie. The book was dedicated to Queen Adelaide, and the subscribers included the Grand Duke of Tuscany, the King of the Belgians, the Dukes of Bedford, Devonshire, Marlborough, Northumberland and Sutherland, the Earls of Burlington, Derby and Powis, Earl Fitzwilliam and Earl Talbot. Although Emperor Nicholas I of Russia was not among the subscribers, a copy did make its way to the Imperial Botanic Garden in Saint Petersburg where it is still the largest book in the library.

Bateman's grandiose *Orchidaceae* duly established his reputation as a botanist and ensured his election as a Fellow of the Royal Society. It might also have been the catalyst for his meeting with Maria Sybilla Egerton-Warburton, the daughter of one of Cheshire's most distinguished families. Happily the Egerton-Warburtons were also a great horticultural dynasty. While Maria herself was an enthusiastic gardener, her brother (nicknamed the 'Great Lilophile') created a notable garden at Arley Hall, and other relations were responsible for the gardens at Tatton Park in Cheshire and Oulton Park in Yorkshire. The pair married in 1838 and lived with his parents in Knypersley Hall, where Bateman landscaped part of the grounds around the elegant eighteenth-century house, creating a fashionably picturesque landscape in the manner prescribed by Uvedale Price (1747–1829). Influential in the early nineteenth century, Price deplored the smoothness of Capability Brown's landscapes and argued instead for the richness and variety of 'unimproved' parkland, promoting a rugged palette of fallen trees, twisted paths, craggy outcrops and textured slopes. At Knypersley, Bateman devised an admirably varied landscape, surrounding a lake to the side of the garden with diverse inlets and promontories, planting mature evergreens to provide instant drama, and adding giant rockworks featuring stones gathered from the Appian Way, Roman tablets and even calcified human bones.

Above: The gardens at Arley Hall, in Cheshire, were created in the 1830s around the newly built Jacobean-style hall by Rowland, Maria Egerton-Warburton's brother. He was nicknamed the 'Great Lilophile', presumably for his love of lilies. While the walled kitchen garden, landscape park and pleasure gardens to the east were relics of the earlier eighteenth-century estate, Egerton-Warburton developed the pleasure garden to the west, creating a long, deep double herbaceous border – one of the first of its kind. To the south of this is an avenue consisting of seven pairs of evergreen or holm oak (*Quercus ilex*) clipped into cylinders.
Right: Hand-coloured lithographic plate after an original by Sarah Anne Drake from James Bateman's ten-volume publication *Orchidaceae of Mexico and Guatemala*.
Right below: From the same book, this plate was drawn by Augusta Withers. She also contributed to some of the volumes of fruit portraits that William Hooker provided for the Royal Horticultural Society as an aid to correct plant identification and naming.

Botanical illustrations have always been an important tool for identifying plants and seeds, particularly as printing processes improved from the earliest woodcuts of the first printed herbals through to the precision of copper-plate engravings. Even after the invention of photography it was many years before colour printing could match the accuracy of botanical illustrations. With their patience and refinement, women were deemed particularly suited to the task, especially as many were prepared to work for little pay and no credit.

William Curtis frequently employed women to do the fiddly work of illustrating and hand colouring the images in his *Botanical Magazine*, for which he paid mere pennies. At a time when women were expected to be modest, many accomplished female artists remained anonymous, simply signing their work 'by a lady'. Nonetheless, illustrating botanical texts was one way women could engage with botany and it is widely believed that these early, female botanical illustrators paved the way for women to take a more active role in the sciences.

Sarah Anne Drake (1803–1857) worked for some of the most famous botanists of the day. Having entered the London house of the botanist John Lindley as a governess, she soon discovered a talent for botanical drawing. After studying botany she began to illustrate Lindley's many books and publications, including his popular two-volume *Ladies' Botany* and his *Sertum Orchidaceum: a wreath of the most beautiful orchidaceous flowers*. Although Drake was largely uncredited for her illustrations, Lindley did name the rare Australian genus of hammer orchids *Drakaea* after her. Drake also illustrated the *Transactions of the Horticultural Society of London* and contributed over 1,000 plates to Sydenham Edwards' *Botanical Register*. Drake's employment ceased in 1847 and little is known about her after this date, although many assume she died of the toxins ingested from her paints – a fate which befell many botanical artists who would lick their brushes to a fine point for depicting delicate details.

Augusta Innes Baker Withers (*c*.1791–1876) was a well-respected botanical artist, known for brilliant use of colour and harmonious compositions. She exhibited at the Royal Academy from 1829 to 1846 and contributed to some of the most important botanical texts of the day. Withers illustrated the whole of *The Pomological Magazine* and provided nearly half of the 250 plates in Benjamin Maund's *The Botanist*. She worked with Drake to illustrate Lindley's *Sertum Orchidaceum* and drew images of fruit for the Royal Horticultural Society. In 1830 she was appointed Flower Painter in Ordinary to Queen Adelaide, but on her royal patron's death Withers' fortunes declined, and when her husband became blind she could not support them both. Too proud to apply to the Artists' Benevolent Fund, Withers instead petitioned Queen Victoria who, in 1864, appointed her Flower and Fruit Painter in Ordinary and bought several of her paintings. Nonetheless Withers had to pawn her work to survive; eventually she was declared bankrupt and died in penury a few years after her husband.

Several years later, after the birth of their second son, the couple moved to Biddulph Grange, 3 kilometres/2 miles from the parental home, though Bateman continued to use the greenhouses at Knypersley. Before the Batemans took it over, Biddulph had served as the local vicarage, having been built on the site of a farm, or grange, attached to a small abbey that was destroyed in Henry VIII's dissolution of the monasteries. Though the Batemans renamed the place Biddulph Grange to reflect its ancient heritage, over the years they transformed it from a modest dwelling into an enormous Italianate mansion, in the style made fashionable by Queen Victoria at Osborne House on the Isle of Wight. As both house and family expanded around him, Bateman embarked on his second magnum opus: the gardens at Biddulph Grange.

In 1847, some years after moving into Biddulph, Bateman met Edward Cooke (1811–1880), a distinguished painter of

LODDIGES: A NEW WORLD OF PLANTS

One of the world's finest commercial nurseries, Loddiges is credited with introducing about 150 plants to Britain. Loddiges was begun in 1771 by Joachim Conrad Loddiges (1738–1826), a German gardener-turned-nurseryman, who had served as apprentice in the gardens of George II in Hanover before emigrating to England during the Seven Years War. One of Loddiges' first introductions was *Rhododendron ponticum* – a dubious distinction in light of its subsequent invasion of the British landscape. Loddiges began his own nursery collection by writing to people around the world, requesting seeds of native plants. His first catalogue, published in 1777, was printed in Latin, English and German. Six years later the catalogue had a foreword in French, indicating the nursery's growing reputation on the Continent. Originally known as Paradise Fields, the nursery changed its name in 1814 to Hackney Botanic Nursery Garden, reflecting a general shift in horticultural inspiration from literature to science. Under Conrad's son, George Loddiges (1786–1846), the nursery provided increasingly exotic material, commissioning plant-hunting expeditions and making good use of Nathaniel Ward's glass cases to transport live plants from around the globe. By the mid-nineteenth century

the nursery covered 6 hectares/15 acres; it had an unparalleled collection of plants as well as a palm house, an arboretum, a rosarium and 300 metres/1,000 feet of hothouses. In 1854 the lease on the land expired, and the family had to cease trading because land values in the region had soared as the city of London expanded northwards.

Left: The marine painter Edward Cooke met James Bateman in 1847, and the pair became friends. Cooke, who was interested in plants, contributed to the gardens at Biddulph Grange by designing many fine architectural features.

Below: Ferns were much appreciated in the early nineteenth century for their fresh greenery. Here they grow at the foot of a short flight of steps leading towards an eerily dark tunnel – one of Bateman's devices for creating a sense of mystery and discovery at Biddulph. To the Victorians, ferns epitomized the mystery of the distant past; after Nathaniel Ward's glass case allowed the transport and housing of ferns, pteridomania – fern fever – swept through Victorian society. In the 1860s alone more than fifty books on ferns were published and by 1891, when the British Pteridological Society was founded, the craze was unabated.

land- and seascapes who also had a keen interest in plants. The two might well have first coincided at Loddiges nursery in Hackney, where Bateman spent many hours browsing for orchids. At the time Edward Cooke lived near the nursery as his father was engraving the plates for Loddiges' monthly publication, the *Botanical Cabinet*. While many of the drawings for the periodical were by Edward's father, some were Edward's and others were drawn by George Loddiges' daughter, Jane, whom Cooke would later marry.

As well as being an accomplished artist, Cooke was a skilled draughtsman and this might be why Bateman invited him to help with the design and layout of the gardens at Biddulph Grange. While Maria undoubtedly advised on the planting, Cooke was responsible for most of the architectural features: garden buildings and rockwork. At that time the Batemans had already fashioned an unusual tunnel fernery leading to the mansion's front entrance. One of Cooke's

first commissions was to design rockwork for this fernery. A passionate geologist, Cooke soon became adept at creating natural-looking rockeries as evidenced in the rocky slopes, boulder-strewn lakesides, grottoes, caves, walls and tunnels underpinning the gardens.

The Batemans' unusual fern tunnel was praised in an article about Biddulph published in the *Gardeners' Chronicle* during 1865, where the writer describes a 'little rocky dell' with a stream flowing beside the entrance path. The article also mentions that rare ferns were housed in illuminated niches set into the enclosing, moss-covered rock wall. While

Below: *Gathering Ferns* by the artist Helen Allingham appeared in the weekly newspaper *The Illustrated London News* in 1871. It shows that collecting ferns was deemed a suitable sport for young men and women to pursue together.

FERN FEVER: A PERMISSIBLE PASSION

Ferns became popular in the early nineteenth century as part of the fashion for exotic plants. While some were imported from abroad, many species were readily available at home, bringing them within the reach of the most humble pteridomaniac. Ferns thrived in the wilder, wetter, peripheral regions of Britain, which were being discovered by aesthetes in search of the picturesque. Fern-hunting was one of the few activities that young men and women could engage in together as it was deemed both healthy and educational. The cultivating of ferns was made much easier when Nathaniel Ward devised his 'closely glazed case' to protect ferns from the sulphuric acid that was released in the burning of coal and polluted Britain's cities. Stylish Wardian cases were soon developed for middle-class drawing rooms, but many fern lovers incorporated grotto-like 'ferneries' or glazed 'fern houses' into their gardens as well. While amateurs might return home with a basket of ferns for private cultivation, fern hawkers plundered the countryside to sell their spoil on street corners. Nineteenth-century 'fern fever' significantly reduced the numbers of several rare native species.

this might seem to present a damp welcome in winter, the magazine's correspondent was clearly enchanted, averring that not even the gayest, scented flowers could present such an agreeable greeting as this choice bit of wild nature, 'with its cool freshness and greenness'.

This exuberant celebration of nature continued from the front entrance into the body of the house. The billiard room's ceiling was glazed to let in the sky, while its full-height windows opened on to a fernery – later transformed into a rhododendron house. The dining room overlooked an open, colonnaded courtyard with climbers growing from the border and clipped shrubs set in coloured sand. The picture gallery had steps leading down to a cool, underground Roman catacomb. A camellia house linked the library and drawing room, while an orangery stretched from the east end of the house to the Geological Gallery at the back. The library itself opened on to the south parterre, and the writing room beside it extended on to the west terrace. On the floor above, a conservatory corridor – featuring exotic fruit trees – led

Below: From upper windows on the south front there was a view of the lake. The gardens evolved over two decades, and by the 1860s the Batemans were opening them to the public. Entry was free from 1–6pm on the first Mondays of the summer months, or at the cost of a shilling on Fridays throughout the year. Those arriving out of hours could apply to the local inn for tickets, with all proceeds going to the Biddulph Old Friendly Society.

from the master bedroom to a first-floor garden entrance. The walls of the main corridor were filled with botanical prints, the library was furnished with botanical books, and no doubt Wardian cases stuffed with plants adorned the drawing rooms and vases of garden flowers filled every available surface. Bateman recommended orchids as table decorations, and was so passionate about his own plants that when staying in London he instructed his gardeners to cut the orchids as they came into bloom and send them on to furnish his hotel rooms.

But it was in the garden that the Batemans really expressed their love of plants. They transformed an unpromisingly bleak moorland site into an eclectic assembly of horticultural exotica. Though undeniably unique, the result was also typically Victorian in its huge range of plant material, its eccentric buildings and its technical innovations.

Following the fashion of the day, the Batemans kept the area immediately around the house rather formal with parterres, terraces, arches and high yew hedges screening the south front of the building from the lake beyond. The upper terraces brought the garden right up to the house.

Above: Biddulph Grange is an enclosed, inward-looking garden, a deliberately artificial world which makes no connection with the rolling countryside beyond, and certainly no reference to the slag pits, furnaces or smoke-belching chimneys that funded its treasures.

Right top: The grounds around the house are treated formally, with dressed stone balustrades, gravel walks and topiary set within a framework of dense yew hedges. As they extend outwards, the grounds become more informal, with sinewy paths linking the different areas of planting.

Below right: The Mosaic Parterre, so called because the outlines were created by crushed terracotta and yellow grog – a by-product of the local pottery industry.

Below far right: The Italian Garden extends from the library, linking the formal gardens near the house with the informal lines of the lake beyond. It is the terracing, in three levels joined by a series of staircases, that gives this area its name, as the planting here is not particularly Italianate.

They were laid out with interconnecting compartments, of which the design ensured that seasonal displays of flowers could be enjoyed without having to pass through enclosures where flowers were past their prime. The Mosaic Parterre, just beyond the library window, provided year-round interest with neat geometric designs picked out in clipped hedging, framed with coloured gravels and planted up with colourful bulbs. Mrs Bateman's Garden at the eastern end of the top terrace displayed a precocious taste for herbaceous perennials long before Gertrude Jekyll made them fashionable. A formal Italian Garden descended beneath the library window, leading from the Rose Parterre down to a fountain on the lower level. Beyond this stretched the famous Dahlia Walk, a long yew-backed corridor divided into compartments by buttressing hedges, which provided a neutral foil to the strong colours of the flower heads.

On the balustraded terrace below the Dahlia Walk, the Araucaria Parterre contains four hedged beds each displaying a single *Araucaria araucana* (monkey puzzle tree). First introduced from Chile by Archibald Menzies in 1795, the monkey puzzle was re-introduced by William Lobb in the early 1840s and Bateman was one of the first private gardeners to grow them in England. Bateman described these curious trees as 'living

Above: The Italian garden looks up to the Terrace.
Right: Dahlias at Biddulph Grange include yellow 'Summertime'; reddy-pink 'Arabian Night'; purple and white 'Edinburgh'; and white 'My Love'.

DAHLIAS: CONTINUING THE JOURNEY

Native to Mexico and Central America, dahlias were introduced into Europe in the late eighteenth century and named after the Swedish botanist Anders Dahl. The Aztecs used dahlia petals for poultices, made water pipes from the hollow stems and ate the sweet, starchy tubers. Plant hunters introduced dahlias as a food crop, but it was the bright flowers that gained favour with the public. Before the discovery of insulin in 1923, diabetics were given a sugar substitute extracted from dahlia tubers.

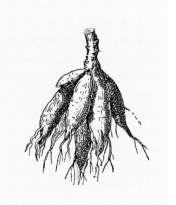

fossils' and preferred them as small specimens; when they became too large for his planting scheme he would move them to the arboretum and replace them with smaller models.

If Biddulph's terrace gardens are rather conventional, the real horticultural innovation lay to the south and east where the garden expands in an unpredictable Alice-in-Wonderland fantasy. Here Bateman played with scale and expectation: enormous trees are raised on mounds to enhance their effect; dark mysterious tunnels lead down blind alleys; low, heavy portals open on to wide meadows. Rockwork, topiary and vegetation are manipulated to guide the unsuspecting visitor through a dream-world of exotic scenes studded with alien plants, outlandish statues and fantastical garden follies. A constantly shifting palette of rocky cliffs, sweeping shrubberies, dense woodland, open ponds, streams and serpentine paths makes the garden seem much larger than its 6 hectares/15 acres. This layout reflects the gardenesque style promoted by

Previous pages: The Dahlia Walk ended in a two-storey viewing pavilion known as the Shelter House.

Left top: The Araucaria Parterre with its four matching monkey puzzle trees.

Left below: A glimpse of the Cheshire Cottage, surrounded by trees, including an older monkey puzzle specimen that outgrew its position in the Parterre.

Right: In a relatively small area Bateman created various microclimates and evoked a myriad of cultures, geographical regions and eras, each separate and distinct, but all skilfully linked to meld and dissolve one into the other without any obvious boundaries or walls. This area was known as Egypt.

Below left: When, after several good years, his prized rhododendrons suddenly failed to flower, Bateman moved them into the fernery and transformed his Himalayan ravine into a Scottish glen. This was filled with ferns, semi–aquatic, marsh and bog plants which thrived in the shady, damp atmosphere created by the artificial stream Bateman induced to run through the area. The mid-nineteenth-century fashion for all things Scottish was inspired by Queen Victoria, who fell in love with Scotland when she first visited in 1842.

Below right: Passing through the stone entrance to the garden known as 'China'.

John Claudius Loudon, a landscape designer and author whose championing of foreign imported plants suited the Victorian craze for novelty. Rejecting the naturalistic style of the previous generation, Loudon felt that gardens should be recognizably artificial; his conviction that the garden's layout should be dictated by the needs of each individual plant led him to create abstract designs with many small raised beds, each designed to display the unique features of a single tree or group of plants.

Like many Victorians, Bateman was an enthusiastic collector of azaleas and rhododendrons. On a crescent-shaped slope at the western edge of the garden he planted them in colour-coordinated bands to create what was known as the 'rainbow'. They were also planted in great masses, interspersed with gigantic heather-covered rocks, to obscure the far edges of the lake. This area was often known as the American Garden, since many of the early rhododendron introductions came from North America.

Above: John Claudius Loudon, the Scottish publisher, designer and garden maker, was one of the most influential horticultural writers of his time, shaping Victorian gardens, both public and private. His seminal *Encyclopaedia of Gardening* remained in print for fifty years after its publication in 1822.

Left below: In the mid-nineteenth century, gardens featuring lime-hating imports such as rhododendrons, azaleas and camellias were often called American gardens, even if they contained species from Turkey, Iran and the Himalayas. This odd nomenclature originates from the collections of American plants that had been fashionable in the eighteenth century, and which tended to contain mainly ericaceous plants.

Right: The Scottish Glen was created by Edward Cooke, a passionate geologist who perfected his rock-working skills by drawing rock formations in Scotland. Originally intended as a Himalayan ravine, it was planted with rhododendrons newly introduced from Sikkim and Bhutan. When the rhododendrons refused to thrive, Bateman and Cooke transformed this area into a Scottish Glen, where they indulged their enthusiasm for ferns, mosses and semi-aquatic plants.

Following pages: One of the garden's great surprises is the area known as 'China'. The ornamental pool is spanned by a wooden footbridge, in a scene framed by rocks and exotic planting including Japanese maples.

Beyond the rhododendron ground visitors found themselves drawn into a vertiginous crag of narrow paths, slippery stepping stones, rocky outcrops and rushing streams. This entirely artificial construct was originally intended to be a Himalayan gorge. Here Bateman attempted to recreate the perfect conditions for his precious rhododendrons, recently imported from Sikkim and Bhutan. When the rhododendrons failed he moved them to the dining-room fernery and planted up the crag – known as the Glen – with mosses, ferns and semi-aquatic plants. At the back of the Glen, a cave beckons; it leads into a long, low, dark tunnel that suddenly emerges into the forecourt of an oriental temple. This is the area known as 'China', a hidden valley completely enclosed from the rest of the garden.

At the heart of 'China' sits a large, still pond which serves as a dazzling mirror to the surrounding slopes. These were carefully planted up with golden larch, purple-leaved acers, hostas, tree peonies, bamboos and other exotica recently introduced from the Far East. Bateman tended to plant in clusters, massing together plants of the same colour or form. Pride of place went to the dramatic, red-leaved Japanese maple, *Acer palmatum* 'Rubrum'; but Bateman was also fond of yellow and purple, which he combined to great effect by placing varieties of golden holly, ivy and yew against purple-leaved elm, beech and hazel. Here Edward Cooke's talents are also demonstrated, in the scale and the quality of his Great Wall of China, a monumental rockwork which encloses the valley. The wall is flanked at one end by a heavy stone watchtower,

Below left and below right: With its layered, upturned roofline embellished with gilded bells, dragons and grebes, this temple is a chinoiserie gem. Inspired by the porcelain, silk and lacquerware imported into Europe from Asia, chinoiserie reached its height in the mid-eighteenth century; Bateman's nineteenth-century Chinese garden allowed him to display his Asian imports in an apparently authentic setting.

Above and right: The willow pattern on a Spode plate inspired the design of the Chinese garden at Biddulph.

and at the other by a delicate, wooden Joss House inspired by humble folk temples where local deities were worshipped. The word 'joss' is a corruption of the Portuguese 'deos', meaning 'God', and came to refer to the incense sticks which were burnt as offerings within.

Other oriental elements include zigzagged wooden fences, a Dragon Parterre cut out of turf and filled in with black coal and red sand, an extraordinary gilded water buffalo with a sphere between its horns – probably inspired by the great bronze ox in Peking's Summer Palace – and an equally extraordinary, gigantic stone frog, which looms over the path. With their vivid, not to say garish colours, these features add a theatrical

Right: The zigzagged chinoiserie fence, vibrantly painted in red, green and yellow.
Below: The Dragon Parterre, an eccentric element in this Victorian vision of the Orient.
Opposite: In the Chinese garden, the gilded water buffalo (top) and monumental frog (below) were crafted by Benjamin Waterhouse Hawkins, as were the sphinxes and ape in the Egyptian Garden.

touch to the garden. While Bateman's 'China' contains all the elements of classical Chinese horticulture – water, rock, buildings and vegetation – ultimately it is more Victorian pastiche than humble place of retreat and reflection.

Leading away from 'China', a meandering path suddenly descends into a dark, sinister cutting. This is the Stumpery, a narrow chasm planted with dead tree roots. Some of these emerge from the ground like twisting limbs to create a rough frame for vines and ferns, others tower 3 metres/10 feet high, merging overhead to create a gnarled tunnel of decomposing vegetation. Stumperies, like rockeries, were a short-lived Victorian vogue, popularized by the desire for picturesque roughness. The path soon ascends from this ominous hollow, leading on to the garden's other great surprise: 'Egypt'. Also a theatrical set piece, 'Egypt' consists of a small rectangular courtyard, tightly concealed behind high beech hedges and guarded by a pair of sphinxes. At the centre of this complex, a clipped yew pyramid encloses an Egyptian Temple. The winged symbol of the Sun God Ra presides over the lintel, and a large stone carving of the ape Thoth, Egyptian god of wisdom, writing and science, greets those who enter the eerie passage.

Above: A stumpery is similar to a rockery, but is made of stumps, logs, bark and other parts of dead trees. Here the stumps were placed into 3-metre/ 10-foot walls flanking a meandering path. The stumpery at Biddulph Grange is thought to be the first in England and it sparked a vogue for these curious features.

Right top: Egyptian motifs became fashionable in the early nineteenth century, after Napoleon's 1798 Egyptian campaign and the subsequent British expedition to remove him. Sir John Soane promoted the architectural style and it was popularized by the Egyptian-inspired building William Bullock had built in Piccadilly to display his collection of curiosities. Egyptian artefacts at the Great Exhibition of 1851 provided further inspiration and the vogue for all things Egyptian peaked in the 1860s, when Thomas Cook began offering tours of the Nile.

Right: The steady stare of a sphinx, its mighty lion's paws covered with leaves from the beech hedge alongside.

Far right: Within the Egyptian garden, enthroned and grimacing, the ape-god Thoth is bathed in an ethereal glow from the ruby-coloured glass above.

Visitors following the passage through the pyramid emerge, unexpectedly, beside a wood-framed chalet. Though known as the Cheshire Cottage in honour of Maria Bateman's origins, this fits into the motif of the Swiss chalet that became a fashionable garden embellishment in the early nineteenth century when Grand Tourists, deterred by the Napoleonic wars from following the usual itinerary through Europe, discovered the delicious terrors of the Swiss Alps. Follies of this sort were often placed in alpine settings, and Biddulph's chalet, with its flanking stone pine cones, duly introduces the Pinetum. Along with his orchids and azaleas, Bateman was passionate about conifers and justly proud of his collection, which was one of the finest in the country. He carefully monitored the soil, drainage and shade levels to ensure the best possible conditions for

Left: The front of the wood-framed Cheshire Cottage bears the initials J and MB to commemorate James and Maria Bateman. The house itself recognizes Maria's local geographical origins.
Right: The Lime Avenue forms part of the historic route between Biddulph and Congleton and marks the western boundary of the garden.

his prized specimens, which included redwoods, mountain hemlock, Japanese cedars and swamp cypress.

Beyond the Pinetum lies the Arboretum, devoted to unusual trees and shrubs. Stretching east from the Arboretum, the Wellingtonia Avenue provides one of the few formal elements in the garden's overall layout. The long, steep avenue rises dramatically to a large basin, which was transported from Knypersley Hall on the death of Bateman's father. Bateman was one of the first to acquire specimens of wellingtonia (*Sequoiadendron giganteum*) after the tree was introduced from California by the plant hunter William Lobb in 1853. To create a more immediate impact, Bateman

Below: The 250-metre/820-foot Wellingtonia Avenue was restored by the National Trust in the 1990s to reflect Bateman's original scheme of alternating wellingtonias and deodar cedars. The common name wellingtonia commemorates the Duke of Wellington, who had recently died when the plant was introduced to Britain in 1853. Its scientific name, *Sequoiadendron giganteum*, honours the Cherokee Indian, Sequoyah. He invented a writing system for his Cherokee tribe and introduced them to literacy in early nineteenth-century America.

interplanted his wellingtonias with deodar cedars, intending that these should be removed within twenty years. He left Biddulph too soon to complete this task, and his successor Robert Heath removed the wellingtonias instead of the cedars.

Perhaps the most curious part of Biddulph was the glazed, 30-metre/100-feet long Geological Gallery through which visitors entered the garden. The corridor was divided into seven bays, each of which represented one of the days in the biblical account of creation. Interpreted rather loosely as a journey from the beginning of the universe to the present time, the bays presented rocks and fossils from a series of succeeding geological epochs: Precambrian granite on Day I; the sponges, molluscs and trilobites of the Palaeozoic era on Day II; ferns, mosses and shells on Day III; fossilized tree remains and reptile prints on Day IV; through to the ammonite, dragonfly and ichthyosaurus of the Jurassic period on Day V; and culminating in the turtle, mammoth tusk and wolf relics of the Tertiary period on Day VI. Day VII being the day of rest, it can be assumed that nothing was created on that day, although as the corridor's seventh bay was removed in the 1930s we will never know; some believe that Bateman displayed his beloved orchids there.

Below: The Geological Gallery is where Bateman displayed his rock and fossil collection, laying his specimens out chronologically to chart the evolution of the world from primary chaos to the glories of the present.

Bateman was a devout and evangelical Anglican; his father-in-law was a minister and his wife was deeply and conventionally religious. Despite his fascination with science, Bateman was a resolute creationist, fiercely upholding the biblical account of creation despite increasing evidence supporting the theory of evolution. Though he sent orchids to Charles Darwin for his experiments, Bateman resisted any challenge to the orthodox explanation; indeed, he disliked hybrid plants because they resulted from man's tampering with God's creation. Some people have interpreted his 'world garden' as an assertion that the world was coming to an end, because of his allusions to great civilizations of the past, as well as his mania for collecting antiquities, fossils and rare plants. Certainly his Stumpery has an apocalyptic feel about it, while the

Left: Like many orchid fanciers, Bateman also collected hummingbirds as these tiny creatures were often found in the same habitats as orchids. Introduced to the hobby by the nurseryman George Loddiges, Bateman would commission plant hunters to send back hummingbirds along with their botanical specimens. He kept his collection in the Geological Gallery, which was also known as the Museum.

BATEMAN AND DARWIN

In a pamphlet of 1864, Bateman attempted to explain his creationist creed while challenging the scientific evidence of evolution: 'To the believer, however, the problem is not hard to solve. Ferns and other flowerless plants came early in the Divine programme, because the coal, into which they were to be ultimately converted, had need to be long accumulating for the future comfort and civilisation of our race; while the genesis of Orchids was postponed until the time drew near when Man, who was to be soothed by the gentle influence of their beauty . . . was about to appear on the scene.'

Above: Darwin's *On the Origin of Species,* published in 1859, promoted the theory of natural selection. Challenging the Christian belief that God made the earth in seven days, Darwin posited the scientific theory that all species descend from a common ancestor, but evolved into different species over millennia, through mutation and adaptation. This conflicted with the teaching of the church, which held that humans were unique and unrelated to other animals.

buffalo, dragons and frogs of 'China' could evoke aspects of the Book of Revelations. However, it is likely that Bateman, as an evangelist, would have made his message clear if this was indeed how he intended the garden to be interpreted. Furthermore, the idea of depicting different civilizations in a single garden was not unique. The nearby estate of Alton Towers boasted a Swiss cottage, a Stonehenge, a Chinese Pagoda Fountain, a Greek monument and Dutch and Alpine gardens; farther away, Woburn Abbey had an American garden, a Chinese dairy and a Thornery among its many eccentric delights; and even Sir Frank Crisp's later creation of Friar Park in Oxfordshire, with its Italian, French, Dutch and Japanese gardens, demonstrates that the idea of a 'world garden' remained potent right up to the end of the century.

Despite its strange and wonderful set pieces, Biddulph was also a family garden. It had a bowling green, a quoit ground, a fives court, a tennis lawn, a music house and rowing boats on the large lake to amuse the four Bateman children. For those of a more romantic bent there was also a 44-hectare/108-acre deer park which Bateman restocked in 1857, and in 1863 he purchased a neighbouring estate to create a woodland walk, complete with picturesque mill, stream, cottage and the ruins of an Elizabethan hall which had been destroyed by parliamentarians in the Civil War.

When he was not busy expanding his garden, Bateman continued to write about orchids. In 1862 and 1863 he contributed a series on the history of orchid cultivation in England to the *Gardeners' Chronicle*; there followed in subsequent years *A Guide to Cool-Orchid Growing*, a *Monograph of Odontoglossum* and *A Second Century of Orchidaceous Plants*. In 1863 Bateman submitted a design for the University Parks in Oxford; it was accepted, and despite modifications, the layout (if not the planting) remains as Bateman intended.

In the late 1860s, just when Biddulph Grange garden was at its height, the Batemans decided to turn the estate over to their eldest son, John. While they had transformed the site to create a glorious garden, they could not change the climate, and Maria suffered from bronchitis, exacerbated by the damp Staffordshire winds. The Batemans moved south and settled, ultimately, in a small villa in Worthing. Their son, having discovered that the estate was heavily mortgaged, sold Biddulph Grange to the local

Left top: In Mrs Bateman's garden, the nanny looks after four children from the Heath family. The Heaths bought Biddulph Grange from James Bateman's son, John, and remained the owners until 1922.
Left below: In 1896, twenty-five years after the Batemans had sold Biddulph Grange, the house was destroyed by a fire. This image shows a fire engine pumping water from the lake while firemen and estate workers look on. The photograph was taken after the event and flames were painted in for dramatic effect.

MP, Robert Heath. He and his son after him maintained the gardens with more diligence than enthusiasm, and after the house was destroyed by fire in 1896 it was rebuilt in the heavy, English neo-baroque style which has remained to this day.

After the First World War, when it was no longer possible to maintain large estates and elaborate gardens, the house was converted into a hospital. The upper gardens were built on, the lower gardens simplified and the wider estate succumbed to neglect and vandalism. Nonetheless Biddulph's reputation endured, and in 1988, when the hospital sold the property, the National Trust took on the grounds of Biddulph Grange and restored them with meticulous care. Using descriptions, photographs and excavations they recreated the original layout and rebuilt many of the pavilions. While some trees and shrubs were added to screen out modern developments, the Trust used only plants available in Bateman's time. With its picturesque buildings, extensive rock-work, pinetum, arboretum, shrubbery and stumpery, today Biddulph Grange remains one of Britain's most complete Victorian gardens.

JANE LOUDON AND THE RISE OF THE LADY GARDENER

An illustration from Jane Loudon's *Botany for Ladies* (1842), which made the scientific study of plants accessible and interesting for beginners.

Jane Loudon (1807–1858) began writing science fiction at the age of seventeen, when her father's death left her orphaned and penniless. Her novel *The Mummy*, published anonymously in 1827, caught the attention of John Claudius Loudon who was intrigued by its description of a steam-driven plough. Though surprised to discover that the author was a woman, within six months he had married her. Jane Loudon helped with her husband's horticultural research, but as she attempted to learn about botany and gardening she was struck by the absence of books for genuine novices. Passing on her own new-found learning, she began to write on gardening for literate, intelligent, interested readers who were not schooled in the sciences. Inspired by the distinguished botanist John Lindley, who was promoting gardening as a fit hobby for women, Jane Loudon directed her books specifically at the ladies' market. Her easy anecdotal style, infectious enthusiasm and beautiful illustrations made these works an immediate success. When her husband died of lung cancer in 1843, leaving her with a ten-year-old daughter to support, Loudon supplemented her books with magazine writing and editing. Though she died, virtually penniless, at the age of fifty-one, Jane Loudon was responsible for making gardening an acceptable, accessible and pleasurable hobby for women.

JOSEPH PAXTON AND THE GREAT EXHIBITION

Above: Inventor Joseph Paxton rose from gardener's boy to knight of the realm.
Below: Inside the Crystal Palace was this Egyptian Hall.
Left: One of two sphinxes guarding 'Egypt'.

When no viable structure had been found by the organizers of the Great Exhibition of 1851, Paxton stepped in with his proposal for a Crystal Palace. Inspired by the structure of *Victoria amazonica*, a giant water lily, and spurred on by the removal of the glass tax in 1845, Paxton's prefabricated glass-and-steel structure required 4,500 tons of iron and 293,000 panes of glass; yet it took a mere eight months to erect. Deemed an architectural marvel and an engineering triumph, the building itself became an enduring emblem of the Great Exhibition, which had been conceived as a way to showcase Britain's superiority in industry and culture. With its mature trees, gushing fountains and many statues, the Crystal Palace was like a winter garden. While Karl Marx dismissed it as a capitalist fetishizing of commodities, 6 million people visited – a third of Britain's population - and the exhibition generated enough surplus money to fund the Victoria and Albert Museum, the Science Museum and the Natural History Museum. His inspired design for the Crystal Palace earned Paxton a knighthood. After the exhibition, the palace was moved to Sydenham Park in south London; in 1936 it burned to the ground.

JOSEPH PAXTON AT CHATSWORTH

One of the great inspirations to nineteenth-century horticulture was the garden at Chatsworth, fashioned from 1826 to 1858 by the 6th Duke of Devonshire and his head gardener Joseph Paxton. Reflecting the horticultural fashions of the time, they created a grand rockery, an arboretum, a pinetum and an azalea dell to house the new specimens introduced by the early plant hunters – many of whom had been sponsored by the Duke himself. They also produced the largest fountain in the world, which emerged from a huge lake to shoot a water-jet 90 metres/295 feet into the air. Fascinated with industrial technology, Paxton exploited new techniques in iron- and glass-making to create a series of greenhouses for the Duke's exotic fruits, ornamentals and orchids. In 1837 he created the Great Stove: the largest conservatory in the world, it covered one-third of a hectare/three-quarters of an acre, and was heated by eight boilers with 11 kilometres/7 miles of iron pipe. Paxton also designed a lily house to accommodate *Victoria amazonica*, a gigantic water lily which he managed to bring into flower for the first time in England, thirteen years after the seeds were introduced to Kew from the Amazon in 1836. Paxton went on to design some of the greatest gardens of the day, as well as pioneering England's earliest public parks.

Above: At the time of its creation, Paxton's Great Stove at Chatsworth was the largest glass structure in the world – 69 metres/226 feet long, 37 metres/121 feet wide and 20 metres/67 feet high, it encompassed 2,787 square metres/30,000 square feet of ground space. Eight underground boilers regulated the temperature to create a temperate zone at one end and a subtropical zone at the other. Extremely costly to maintain, it was left unheated through the First World War and all the plants died. It was demolished in the 1920s.

Below left: Paxton's daughter Anne standing on a *Victoria amazonica* leaf in the water lily house at Chatsworth. Paxton was intrigued by the leaf's structure, its rigid radiating ribs providing strength while the cross ribs provided flexibility. This organic structure inspired his design for the Crystal Palace.

Above: The Pagoda at the Royal Botanic Gardens, Kew, on the outskirts of London. This iconic, ten-storey building was designed by Sir William Chambers after his travels in China, and was completed in 1762.

Below right: Waddesdon in Buckinghamshire, with its famous mounded carpet bedding. Keen to surprise and delight his garden visitors, Baron Ferdinand de Rothschild incorporated such entertaining features as an aviary, an ornamental dairy and a menagerie into the garden, but it was his sister and heir who added the three-dimensional carpet bedding for which Waddesdon is best known.

THE ROYAL BOTANIC GARDENS, KEW

The Royal Botanic Gardens, Kew, were one of the major sources of plant material for Bateman and other innovative nineteenth-century horticulturists. Originally a hunting lodge for James I, Kew was a royal residence by the late seventeenth century. In the mid-eighteenth century Augusta, Dowager Princess of Wales, expanded the estate, embellished the grounds with exotic buildings and created a botanic garden. By the end of the century, under the direction of Joseph Banks, Kew contained one of the greatest plant collections in the world. In 1840 the gardens were adopted as a national botanic garden; under the first director, William Hooker, and his son Joseph who succeeded him, the Herbarium and Palm House were built, and Kew became a leading force in the introduction and propagation of plants. Today its 120 hectares/300 acres of gardens and greenhouses hold the world's largest collection of living plants. In the eighteenth century, Lancelot 'Capability' Brown had applied for the position of head gardener at Kew; it is perhaps fortunate that he was turned down.

WADDESDON MANOR AND THE ROTHSCHILDS

Created in the late nineteenth century for Baron Ferdinand de Rothschild, epitomizes the High Victorian style. Purchased in 1874, the grounds were transformed from bare farmland into one of the most opulent gardens of the age. Along with an aviary, a menagerie of deer, goats and llamas, an ornamental dairy, glasshouses and grottoes, Waddesdon was best known for the parterre garden in front of its Loire-château-style manor house. Here displays of carpet bedding would be created with low, brightly-coloured plants forming elaborate designs round the central fountain. At Waddesdon the designs were replaced twice a year, in spring and autumn, with up to 50,000 plants being used in each planting scheme. Carpet bedding was a quintessentially Victorian feature, as wealthy horticulturists attempted to outdo each other in the vibrancy and complexity of their designs. While the practice fell out of favour at the beginning of the twentieth century, it has experienced a revival recently, with respected artists being commissioned to design new bedding schemes.

NYMANS

NYMANS

THE MESSELS' EDWARDIAN RURAL RETREAT

Where the Victorian garden was a celebration of colonial confidence, the Edwardian garden was decidedly more discreet. It celebrated Britishness of a very particular sort – not the arrogance of Empire, but a gentler and more chivalrous idea of nationhood. If the Victorian garden was a proclamation, the Edwardian garden was a retreat. And the most exquisite retreat of them all is Nymans in West Sussex, created over a span of three generations by the Messels, a family of German-Jewish descent.

By the late nineteenth century the certainties of the Victorian age were being severely challenged, as the economic confidence of the early decades gave way to the Long Depression of 1873 to 1896. The Industrial Revolution had seemed to promise unlimited prosperity, growth and opportunity, but bad weather in the mid-1870s led to a succession of poor harvests that undermined prosperity; farmers and landowners were hit even harder when cheap wheat and meat were imported from the Americas. As a result of reduced agricultural wages and unemployment, social unrest spread across rural England. Meanwhile, continental Europe was being rocked by a series of conflicts: the Wars of Italian Independence, the Franco-Prussian War and the Spanish American War.

Even when the weather improved and England's harvests revived, foreign imports continued to be cheaper than home-grown produce. The price of agricultural land dropped, while taxes steadily rose, forcing many landowners to sell their estates. And the people who could afford to buy these estates up came from the newly rich class of financiers, one of whom was Ludwig Messel.

Ludwig was from Darmstadt, capital of the Grand Duchy of Hesse in the centre of modern-day Germany. Born in 1847 into a successful banking family, he was named after the Grand Duke, with whom his family was connected: his grandfather had served Ludwig III as chancellor. In 1866 Hesse joined the Austro-Prussian War on the side of Austria. Even though the conflict lasted only seven weeks,

Left: In the decades after Ludwig Messel first planted the barren hilltop around his Sussex country retreat, Nymans was gradually transformed from open agricultural land into a series of secret garden spaces, deeply embowered in woodland and hedges.

its consequences were profound for the Duchy: Prussia, victorious, annexed parts of Hesse and demanded punitive reparations. The prospects for enterprising young men were thus severely diminished; and so, given that their father had died several years earlier of typhoid, the two eldest Messel brothers decided to emigrate.

Britain seemed a good choice of destination because, in 1862, the Grand Duke's heir had married Queen Victoria's daughter, Princess Alice. While anti-semitism was rife throughout Europe and anti-German feeling almost as strong, at least Britain's reigning queen had German relatives (even if they were openly derided in the press). Besides, by the mid-nineteenth century Britain was the richest and most powerful nation on earth. It was also relatively advanced in political terms. The year 1858 was a landmark in the emancipation of the Jews, with new legislation opening the way for Lionel de Rothschild to take up his seat in the House of Commons and thereby become the first Jewish member of Parliament. Ten years later Benjamin Disraeli, a Christian of Italian-Jewish parents, became prime minister. These events suggested that talented, hard-working Jews could rise unhindered in British society.

Family lore has it that the Messel brothers arrived in England with only a few gold coins sewn into their shirts. But they may been helped through introductions to figures in London's financial world, underpinned as it was by Jewish banking dynasties including the Cassel, Montefiore, Montagu and Rothschild families. Ludwig soon secured a job with the stockbroking firm of Seligman Brothers and in 1869 his younger sister, Lina, whom he had invited over on a visit, was courted by and married the head of the company. Determined to integrate, two years later Ludwig married a woman from classic English stock. Annie Cussans was the daughter of a British army officer whose family fortunes, built on Jamaican sugar plantations, had very likely declined after the abolition of the slave trade in the 1830s. Since Annie's parents had recently both died, there was no one to object to the match. She and Ludwig were married in a Nonconformist chapel and their children were brought up as Christians.

Ludwig soon moved on from Seligman Brothers to establish his own very successful stockbroking firm. Annie had six children; as the family expanded, the Messels moved from Brixton to Kensington, then to Hyde Park, gradually filling their house with the highest-quality furniture, art and books. The boys were sent to Eton and Oxford; the girls sat

Above: Benjamin Disraeli was baptized into the Church of England at the age of twelve, but the fact that someone born a Jew could rise through the British Establishment to become prime minister indicated a level of religious tolerance that would have inspired ambitious young Jewish men, like Ludwig Messel, to emigrate to Britain.

for the finest portrait painters. The most fashionable writers, artists and musicians were invited to dinner. But like many middle-class families, the Messels longed to escape the smoke and crowds of central London.

By the 1890s, the counties south of London were already being dubbed as a 'stockbroker belt' due to the affluent financiers rushing to inhabit the Kentish orchards, Surrey heaths and hilly Sussex Weald. Agriculture had been in decline for several decades so rural property was cheap, and transport was improved by the roads and railways that were pushing ever deeper into the countryside.

Land had always been a sign of rank in British society; but whereas the goal of aspiring Victorians had been a magnificent estate, now the ultimate status symbol was a rural retreat. In 1890 the Messels found Nymans, a 240-hectare/ 600-acre farm in West Sussex. The views were spectacular, with hills rolling south to the Downs and the sea beyond. A railway viaduct in the distance added a classical note. There was a wooded slope to provide the shooting so beloved of Edwardian sportsmen, and a small lake at the bottom offered the gentler pleasures of boating and bathing. On the road leading to the local village stood a gardener's cottage and walled kitchen garden, and at the heart of the estate was

Below: Ludwig and Annie Messel, in old age, on the porch at Nymans. Despite their different cultural backgrounds, Ludwig and Annie had a long, happy and fruitful marriage.

Left: Research into Nymans' past suggests that various South African plants had been trialled in the grounds, which has recently led the National Trust to create a South African bed at the bottom of the garden. A neglected patch was reclaimed and the weeds replaced with prairie-style planting to blend with views over the Weald beyond. Kniphofias are a central feature of the new bed, along with other unusual and attractive plants such as large, daisy-like *Berkheya purpurea* 'Zulu Warrior', purple-hooded *Gladiolus papilio* and autumn-flowering nerines.

a large, rather sombre Regency villa. The house was set within extensive lawns studded with a monkey puzzle tree, a morinda spruce (*Picea smithiana*) and an elegant, sweeping cedar of Lebanon (the only one of the three still standing and now the oldest tree in the garden).

Ludwig purchased the property and immediately hired his youngest brother Alfred, a distinguished architect working in Germany, to renovate the house. Alfred added features deemed essential to any English country gentleman: a large conservatory to the west, a billiard room to the east, and between them a strange three-storey Gothic tower. He later went on to embellish the garden, designing a summer house

FOUNDATION OF THE ROYAL HORTICULTURAL SOCIETY

The Horticultural Society of London was founded in 1804 by the botanist Sir Joseph Banks and the industrialist John Wedgwood. Its avowed purpose was to promote the exchange of horticultural information, to improve horticultural practice, and to provide for the exhibition of plants at flower shows. The society's membership was initially confined to the nobility, aristocracy and landed gentry; however, practical gardeners were given the 'privileges of fellowship' for a reduced fee. In 1809 the society received its first royal charter, becoming the Royal Horticultural Society. In 1822, 13 hectares/33 acres of land were leased on the Duke of Devonshire's estate at Chiswick: the demonstration garden created there was subsequently built over, but its trace remains in the street named Horticultural Place. Meanwhile, the RHS began offering regular meetings, lectures and fortnightly shows of produce in a small hall near its Westminster offices. It also initiated annual 'floral fetes', forerunners of today's internationally renowned RHS Chelsea Flower Show.

The RHS sponsored scientific research into such areas as genetics and fertilizers in its early years, and also financed several successful plant hunters, including David Douglas. In 1842 the society appointed Robert Fortune to collect on its behalf in China, furnishing him with a wish list that included mandarins, double yellow roses, different kinds of tea and the peaches grown in the emperor's Peking garden (said each to weigh two pounds, or roughly one kilogram). However, in the

Sir Joseph Banks (left) and John Wedgwood (right)

1850s the RHS fell on hard times and was obliged to sell off its library and herbarium. In 1861, under the presidency of Prince Albert, it was granted a new royal charter. In 1866 it purchased the library of its former secretary, John Lindley, and began to rebuild its collection of botanical texts. Then in 1903 it was given the Surrey estate of Wisley as an experimental garden and the following year, after a successful appeal for funds, the society opened new offices and an exhibition hall, Lindley Hall, on Vincent Square in Westminster. Today the Lindley Library Trust holds 50,000 books, 1,500 periodicals and 18,000 drawings; and the RHS as a whole is involved in many different activities: it sets exams for student gardeners, sponsors various specialist publications, advises many organisations on the management of historic gardens, and administers the annual Britain in Bloom competition.

in the form of a Greek temple and a viewing platform, called 'the Prospect', extending over the valley to the east.

Garden making was the key to social integration in that particular corner of England. The Messels' nearest land-owning neighbour was Wilfred Loder, whose garden at The High Beeches boasted magnificent woodland, water gardens and wildflower meadows. His brother, Sir Edmund Loder, an expert botanist, breeder of rhododendrons and big-game hunter, was busy creating a wildlife park at Leonardslee, near Horsham. A stalwart supporter and early council member of the Royal Horticultural Society, it was probably Sir Edmund who in 1888 sponsored Ludwig's election as fellow to the society (as members were then called).

Among Nymans' other neighbours with notable gardens was the distinguished naturalist Frederick Du Cane Godman, whose garden at South Lodge in Horsham was known for its collections of alpines, orchids, rhododendrons and many rare, beautiful plants. Nearby were also Wakehurst Place, with its ornamental garden and extensive woodlands; Borde Hill, which would ultimately boast nine different garden rooms; and Sheffield Park with its elegant eighteenth-century landscape. A little to the north-east of Nymans lay the Elizabethan manor of Gravetye, which garden writer William Robinson had recently purchased and where he was

Right: Gravetye Manor, in West Sussex, was from 1884 the home and testing ground of William Robinson, outspoken champion of wild and natural garden styles. This corner of south-east England was a hotbed of horticultural innovation at the time, as garden makers at Borde Hill, Sheffield Park, High Beeches, Wakehurst Place and Leonardslee competed to obtain the latest plant introductions, to hybridize new forms and to develop novel approaches to garden design. Their zeal and friendly rivalry spurred Ludwig on in his own horticultural ventures.

ROBERT FORTUNE: ADVENTURES IN ASIA

Robert Fortune (1812–1880) was a Scottish gardener and botanist who was sent by the Royal Horticultural Society to collect plants in China in the wake of the 1842 Treaty of Nanking, which marked the end of the First Opium War and opened the country to Western trade. On this first expedition, Fortune spent nearly three years visiting the European treaty ports along the coast to purchase material from gardens and nurseries. He also overcame the restrictions placed upon European visitors, who were only permitted one day's travel inland, by disguising himself as a Chinese merchant. Since the southern areas had already been well covered, he headed for the rich plains of northern China, where he collected tree peonies and kumquats, among other finds. Fortune mounted two further expeditions for the East India Company. He was the first westerner to realize that green and black tea came from the same plant, and it was he who shipped the plants that established India's tea industry. In 1860 Fortune travelled to Japan to report on silk manufacture and rice growing. During his career he transformed English horticulture by introducing more than 100 plants, including daphnes, wisterias, primulas and weigelas. He is remembered in the names of many favourite garden plants, such as *Hosta fortunei*, *Trachycarpus fortunei* and *Saxifraga fortunei*.

WILLIAM ROBINSON: PIONEER OF THE WILD GARDEN

William Robinson (1838–1935), born in Ireland, was a self-taught botanist, gardener, designer and journalist, who became one of the most influential horticulturists of the twentieth century. Having started his career as garden boy to the Marquess of Waterford, he soon moved on to the Royal Botanic Society's garden in Regent's Park, London. In the 1860s Robinson began writing for the *Gardeners' Chronicle*, later launching two publications of his own that would cater to the growing middle-class interest in garden making: *The Garden* in 1871 and *Gardening Illustrated* in 1879. Of the many books he also published, the most popular, *The Wild Garden* (1870), owed much of its success to the delightful illustrations by Alfred Parsons. Through his writing and the garden he created at Gravetye Manor, West Sussex, Robinson championed a

naturalistic approach – and won many followers. He deplored the artifice of High Victorian formality, with its topiary, standard roses, hothouse exotics, bedding out, waterworks and statuary. In their place, Robinson promoted the use of native plants, hardy perennials, ground cover, creepers, ramblers, bulbs, and alpines. His espousal of native British flora, of naturalization and of an informal, cottage-garden style found an appreciative audience with those whose tastes were shaped by the Arts and Crafts movement.

pioneering an unorthodox 'natural' approach to gardening. Challenging the distinction between garden and landscape, Robinson happily mixed British native plants with exotics, while encouraging indigenous flora to flow through the garden. Controversially, he cut down some fashionable but imported wellingtonias to replace them with natives.

In the early years of the twentieth century William Robinson became a regular visitor to Nymans – and he would have been generous with advice. His free-form style influenced the wider layout of the garden, and is evident in the wildflower glades which dot the woodlands. But Ludwig was not adventurous or confident enough to adopt the Robinsonian approach fully. Nor did Nymans have the unifying plan of a grand formal garden. Rather, it evolved over time, its series of distinct areas, each with its own planting and mood, loosely linked together to create a romantic, harmonious whole.

Although the Messels were well versed in the arts and sciences, they were less familiar with the stuff of horticulture. Before they could master this quintessentially English hobby, they would first need to find some expert help. James Comber was a local farmer's son, who had been employed at various Sussex estates before being apprenticed to the London nursery of James Veitch & Sons. In 1895, at the age of twenty-nine, Comber accepted the post of head gardener at Nymans: the pay was good, the owner interested, and there was clearly money for improvements. As for the challenges of the site, the hilltop garden was exposed, but at least the frost rolled downhill and the land was fertile and free-draining.

In many ways it was a marriage of opposites: Ludwig was short, dark and spoke with a heavy German accent; Comber was tall, thin and descended from generations of solid yeoman stock. Nonetheless, the two men respected each other and worked well together. Comber's horticultural expertise was balanced by Ludwig's aesthetic sensibility. For while he had little time for hobbies, Ludwig loved music and art, being an exuberant collector of paintings and a talented watercolourist with a good eye for colour and design. Over the next two decades this extremely successful partnership

Above: James Comber spent most of his working life as head gardener at Nymans. In the years before the First World War, he was in charge of ten garden staff. His position carried with it both considerable responsibility and prestige, enabling him to rise in social status above his origins as a farmer's son.

Right top: The Sunk Garden, with Italianate, 1920s loggia and central stone urn, has recently been redeveloped by the National Trust. Its sunken nature provides intimacy, and also adds variety to the open, horizontal plane of the main lawn. As Sunk Gardens were popular in the Messels' day, they may have been inspired by the example created at Kensington Palace in 1908, or the Great Plat at Hestercombe.

Right below: Nymans sits on a hilltop 137 metres/ 450 feet above sea level, with spectacular views on three sides. The landscape rolls gently to the South Downs, with Brighton and the sea beyond.

Below: Remarkable trees at Nymans: this venerable cedar of Lebanon (below) was one of the few mature trees in the garden when the Messels purchased the estate in 1890. Incredibly, it survived the great storm of 1987, which uprooted other trees nearby. The Pinetum (bottom) was developed as a collection of rare conifers, but can be enjoyed simply for its many shades of green. In another area (right), an impressive *Sequoiadendron giganteum* (giant redwood or wellingtonia) towers over people and plants alike.

created what was to become one of England's most glorious and best-loved gardens.

Comber's initial priorities were practical. He concentrated on the kitchen garden, orchard, cutting garden and conservatory. On any country estate the head gardener was expected to provide great vases of cut flowers every morning, along with a succession of hothouse plants in pots to adorn the house. He also had to provide enough fresh fruit and vegetables to feed the family, staff and guests, with a surplus to supply the London residence as well. Under Comber's stewardship, Nymans acquired a peach house and two vineries, for crops of both early- and late-fruiting grapes; other glasshouses were dedicated to strawberries, melons, figs and tomatoes. Hardier fruit trees were trained along the kitchen-garden walls to benefit from their warmth, and soft fruit bushes planted at the base. Once Comber had the utilitarian gardens in hand, he and Ludwig began transforming the several acres of indifferent pleasure grounds.

One of their first additions was the Pinetum, which they laid out in a grand horseshoe curve to the north of the house. Essential not only as a fashionable feature, the Pinetum at Nymans also served a very specific function: it created a dense shelter belt to screen house and garden from the bitter north-east winds. Many different varieties of pine, thuja, sequoia, cedar, juniper and cypress were planted, then surrounded by a protective band of faster-growing spruce. Next they laid out the Arboretum, extending eastwards down the hill from the Pinetum. Here they experimented with nine different species of eucalyptus, fast-growing evergreen trees first introduced to Britain from Tasmania in the eighteenth century. Among other treasures were *Nyssa sylvatica* (tupelo), *Liquidambar styraciflua* (sweet gum) and *Tilia americana* (American lime), all native to America.

Closer to the house, the lawns and pleasure grounds were contained within a ha-ha. To the north, an old walled orchard was turned into a simple cottage-style garden. A modest sundial was stationed at the centre, herbaceous borders were planted along the main path, lilies and primulas sheltered in the corners, and clematis and roses were set to ramble through the ancient apple trees in the manner recommended by Gertrude Jekyll.

The Rose Garden that Comber and Ludwig created was surrounded by a belt of shrubs, again for shelter. They filled it with Hybrid Teas and climbing roses, including the fashionable semi-evergreen, delicately white-flowered *Rosa wichurana*. Beyond this, near the tennis lawn, a croquet lawn was cut into the slope. The resulting rock face provided the opportunity for a rock garden to be constructed by the fashionable firm of Pulham & Son. The company's reputation had risen earlier in the century when James Pulham invented Pulhamite, a mixture of cement and rubble sculpted to form artificial rocks. They often used a combination of Pulhamite and real rocks to build the grottoes and follies so popular at the time, but the Rock Garden at Nymans was formed solely from natural stone. This area was planted with shrubs such as cotoneasters and certain veronicas, along with tough, low-growing flowering plants such as rock roses and aubretias.

Beyond the Rock Garden, in the sandy loam of the heath, large rocks were positioned and hillocks sculpted to create a heather garden. It was planted with a spectrum of heathers ranging through white, mauve and crimson, accompanied by pieris and prostrate forms of rhododendron. Dwarf mountain pines were situated to protect the heather from winter wind and snow. While it was not uncommon at the time for heather to be used as ground cover beneath conifers, Nymans' Heather Garden is thought to be the first example of an area dedicated to this group of plants. Messel embellished the planting a few years later with stone lanterns and ornamental railings, for an oriental feel. This mood was enhanced by the long pergola built along the western edge of the croquet lawn, featuring *Wisteria sinensis* (Chinese wisteria), whose profuse, early-flowering racemes made it an instant success when introduced in the early nineteenth century. Roses, honeysuckle and clematis brought colour to the pergola in summer.

From the pleasure grounds, a curving avenue of limes led towards the Pinetum. Beyond this lay the steeply sloping

Above: Inspired by the heathers he had seen growing near King William's Temple at the Royal Botanic Gardens, Kew, Ludwig decided to create a heather garden at Nymans. The chosen ground was sculpted into hillocks and planted with fifty varieties of winter-flowering *Erica* and late-summer flowering *Calluna vulgaris*.

GERTRUDE JEKYLL: THE QUEEN OF SPADES

Gertrude Jekyll (1843–1932), an artist, author, nurserywoman and garden designer, is said to have changed the face of England more than anyone except Capability Brown. Born in the year that John Claudius Loudon died, Jekyll trained as an artist in the South Kensington School of Art in London. A deterioration in her eyesight forced her, when in her thirties, to turn from painting to gardening, where she applied scientific theories on colour to garden planting. Famed for her subtle colour harmonies and dramatic use of complementary colours, Jekyll was also the first to promote single-colour borders. Although known for her long collaboration with the architect Edwin Lutyens, whose austere classical layouts she would soften with luxuriant planting, Jekyll's earliest horticultural influence was William Robinson, champion of wild and woodland gardening. She lived in an era when gentlewomen were not expected to charge money for their designs, but nevertheless ran a prosperous nursery supplying the many plants required for her complex garden plans. As well as publishing over 1,000 articles and writing more than a dozen garden books, she also provided designs for over 400 gardens – many of which she never actually visited, working, instead, from site plans and soil samples. The first woman ever to receive the RHS Victoria Medal of Honour, Jekyll was also awarded the RHS' prestigious Veitch Memorial Medal for outstanding contributions to the art, science or practice of horticulture.

woodland, its entrance marked by Alfred Messel's Greek Temple. Here, beneath the native beech, oak and ash, were carpets of bluebells; wildflower meadows filled the more open parts. Paths threaded down to the lake (created before the Messels' time, probably for iron smelting). Filled with golden carp, the lake was a favourite spot for picnics and bathing; and in winter there was skating.

As the children grew up, Nymans became popular among the younger generation for its spirited house parties. Whenever the boys came home from boarding school and, later, university, the girls, who were educated at home, ensured weekends and holidays full of fun and games. In 1897 Leonard, the eldest son, proposed to Maud Sambourne, who was the daughter of one of his father's friends. Edward Linley Sambourne, a cartoonist for the prestigious magazine *Punch*, had absorbed the Messels into his artistic London circle; the two wives were friends and their offspring had played together as children. Despite these ties, and regardless of the Messels' greater wealth, Leonard's offer was not greeted with unmitigated delight. The Sambournes were archetypically English in their attitudes, and anti-semitism was still a major force in English society. Even though the Messel children had been brought up as Christians, the family would be regarded as Jewish for many generations. Finally, however, Maud accepted and the couple married the following year, although Maud's mother despaired that their children might look 'too Hebrew'.

Above: Leonard Messel and Maud Sambourne were childhood neighbours who reconnected as young adults, when Leonard returned to England after several years working in a bank in Germany. He found that Maud had blossomed in the interval, but his impetuous offer of marriage was summarily rejected. He persisted, Maud eventually conceded, and their marriage proved to be long and contented.

In 1889 Annie Messel had given birth to a late and unexpected daughter, Muriel. As the youngest child by more than a decade, Muriel got little companionship from her older siblings. She attached herself instead to her father who, in his retirement, was becoming increasingly obsessed with his garden. From him she gained an understanding of design, and from Comber learnt a great deal about best horticultural practice. Not surprisingly, Muriel in time became an expert gardener and went on to put her stamp on the grounds. She is particularly associated with the herbaceous borders that flanked the paths in the Wall Garden. In 1905 a journalist writing about Nymans in *Garden Life* mentions a noble herbaceous border 'a hundred yards long and twelve feet wide' (about ninety by four metres). If Muriel did indeed

Left: Ludwig, possibly with his youngest daughter, Muriel. While rather remote and stern with his older children, Ludwig had softened by the time Muriel arrived. She was the apple of her father's eye, and under his tutelage became an expert gardener. Muriel grew up to be extremely independent, owning a car long before it was fashionable for women to drive, but she died before she reached thirty.

design this border, it indicates her horticultural prowess at the tender age of sixteen.

Herbaceous borders supplanted ornate Victorian bedding parterres towards the end of the nineteenth century, but they are by nature ephemeral and most did not survive the labour shortages of the First World War – as was the case at Nymans. Some black-and-white photographs in the family archive attest to the vibrancy of Nymans' borders, but no planting plans remain to indicate what exactly was growing there. It is highly likely that the borders were influenced by the work of Gertrude Jekyll, who typically arranged diagonal drifts of perennials by colour and size, so that as one drift finishes flowering it can be cut back, leaving the neighbouring drifts to billow forth and fill the gap. This requires considerable skill and plant knowledge to create, and a good deal of labour to maintain.

As the shelter belts became denser over the years, Ludwig and Comber began to experiment with camellias, azaleas, rhododendrons and Himalayan plants, massing them in acidic

Below and on following pages: Oliver Messel's painting (below) shows the Herbaceous Borders in summer, the wide path leading to topiary and a fountain. Family lore held that it was Muriel who presided over these famous borders, and that they were planned and planted with the advice of Nymans' neighbour, William Robinson. The borders today (following pages) are planted in colourful tiers, with perennials, dahlias and annuals reaching their peak in July and August.

soil on the banks below the Pinetum and Arboretum. In 1902, when plant hunter Ernest Henry Wilson returned from the first of his Veitch-sponsored expeditions to China, Comber's previous employment with the nursery would have ensured that Nymans had the pick of new introductions. Spurred on by his successes, and the admiration of his gardening neighbours, Ludwig was constantly seeking underused garden spaces to test out new species.

Since the Wall Garden offered warmth and shelter for his exotic plants, Ludwig began transforming this sleepy cottage garden into a grand showpiece. The modest sundial was replaced with a marble fountain urn, and the four surrounding yews were clipped into eccentric chess-piece shapes; a semicircular flight of steps was added and the entrance embellished with a carved stone archway. Glasshouses were constructed north of the Wall Garden to nurture new specimens before they were released to the cold ground. When Ernest 'Chinese' Wilson introduced the spectacular *Davidia involucrata* (handkerchief tree), Nymans obtained one of the first, precious seedlings; planted in the Wall Garden in 1908, it took seven long years to flower. Visitors were also amazed by the huge, waxy pink flowers of *Magnolia campbellii*, the size of dinner plates; by the distinctive peeling bark of stewartia; and by the delicate, rose-like flowers of eucryphia, a tree originating from the southern hemisphere. While these tests of hardiness were successful, many were not. William Robinson later praised Ludwig's courageous – even reckless – willingness to undertake the most daring experiments.

Nonetheless, the Wall Garden was soon overflowing and a new space, the Top Garden, was brought into cultivation. Flanked by a pair of tall cypresses rising from an azalea thicket, this area soon boasted great banks of flowering shrubs: the discreet but divinely scented osmanthus, red-flowered dogwood, winter-flowering witch hazels and pretty pink *Kolkwitzia* (beauty bush).

Above: Making use of the shelter from maturing trees to experiment with rare and exotic species, Ludwig planted tender rhododendrons arriving from China and Sikkim – that mysterious landlocked Indian state in the heart of the Himalayas.

Although Ludwig consistently refused to exhibit at the regular RHS shows, he was happy to share his treasures with an appreciative audience and through the early twentieth century Nymans clearly held its own in horticultural Sussex. A guest book of the time lists several garden luminaries: Miss Ellen Ann Willmott, plantswoman and tireless champion of roses; the painter Alfred Parsons, who had illustrated books for both Willmott and William Robinson; Richard Irwin Lynch of Cambridge University Botanic Garden; R.L. Harrow from the Royal Botanic Garden Edinburgh; William Jackson Bean of the Royal Botanic Gardens, Kew, specialist in trees and shrubs; the expert Cornish gardeners J.C. Williams, P.D. Williams and Arthur Townshend Boscawen; and Arthur Dorrien-Smith of Tresco Abbey Gardens in the Isles of Scilly.

In the early years of the twentieth century, as the political situation in Europe slowly disintegrated, Nymans became a sanctuary. The unification of Germany in the late nineteenth century had presented a brash and dangerous prospect and, as the threat of war increased, anti-German feeling infused all elements of English life. Even though Ludwig had taken British citizenship and felt completely integrated, suddenly he and his family were seen as the enemy. In 1913, to counter her father's increasing depression, Muriel convinced him to help her compile a list of Nymans' plant collections. She was inspired in this by Sir Edmund Loder's recent catalogue for Leonardslee. The work of cataloguing went some way to distracting Ludwig from the worsening situation, but when war was declared he succumbed to illness and despair. Had he known that his son would be distinguished

Below: *Kolkwitzia amabilis,* named after the German botanist Richard Kolkwitz, was introduced to Britain by Ernest 'Chinese' Wilson' in 1901. It first flowered at the Exeter nursery of James Veitch & Sons in 1910, and in 1923 it won an Award of Merit when presented to the RHS by Nymans. *Kolkwitzia amabilis* was one of the special shrubs Ludwig made space for in the Top Garden.

with an OBE and that his great-grandson would marry into the British royal family, it might have lessened his anguish; but in 1915 Ludwig Messel died, and the family believed it was of a broken heart.

The Nymans' plant list was less than half-finished when Ludwig died. Muriel devoted herself to the task of completing the catalogue as a tribute to her father. In 1918 *A Garden Flora* was published by *Country Life* magazine. With an introduction by William Robinson and ten illustrations by Alfred Parsons, the catalogue contained an alphabetical list of more than 2,000 plants growing at Nymans, with brief notes on the unusual species.

The First World War was a difficult time for all garden owners, but along with the usual staff shortages and the absence of materials, the Messels had to contend with some virulent anti-German propaganda. The Messel boys were unable to serve overseas, because of their heritage, and were instead pressed into service training recruits. Leonard rose to the rank of lieutenant colonel, a title he retained for

Left top: In old age, Ludwig Messel became increasingly distressed at the prospect of a major European war and yet failed to move large investments in Russia and Germany to a safer place. As a result, the family suffered enormous financial losses in the First World War, although these were soon recovered.

Left below: The Heather Garden and pergola in a painting by Alfred Parsons, who illustrated *A Garden Flora* (1918). At the end of the book, which catalogues the plants grown at Nymans and was published as a tribute to Ludwig Messel, Muriel describes her father's garden as 'the triumph of hope'.

Above: Leonard Messel was involved in the military Volunteer Movement as a young man, and joined the British army in 1914. Debarred from service overseas due to his German descent, he raised and trained the 4th Reserve Battalion of the Buffs (Royal East Kent Regiment), attaining the rank of lieutenant colonel.

the rest of his life, and was awarded an OBE for his contribution to the war effort. But the end of the war did not mark the end of the Messels' troubles. In 1918 Muriel died in the influenza pandemic that killed more civilians than the war. Soon after Muriel's death, her sister-in-law died in childbirth and several years later, unable to cope with the loss of his wife, her brother Harold committed suicide. In 1920 Annie Messel died, as did Ludwig's brother Rudolph, a brilliant chemist who had never married but was much loved by the family.

Nymans passed to the next generation and entered a new incarnation in the hands of Leonard and Maud Messel. To Leonard's surprise, Maud and their three children refused to move to Nymans until he agreed to tear down the heavy Germanic house and replace it with something more fashionable. Maud envisioned a vaguely Arts and Crafts stone manor house, with a suggestion of monastic origins. That unsettled, post-war period was dominated by nostalgia; with its vernacular architecture and honest craftsmanship, the Arts and Crafts movement provided an idealized image of rural life, simple and pious, untouched by the ruthless industry and brutal mechanization which had operated so effectively in the trenches. The old house at Nymans was duly torn down. The main entrance was switched to the east so that visitors could appreciate the magnificent views across the valley. An entrance courtyard was created, with an arched gateway and a lantern-topped dovecote in the corner. The design for the house included steeply pitched roofs, tall chimneys, mullioned windows and stone porches; this Elizabethan flavour was reinforced inside with beamed ceilings, large fireplaces, low doors and narrow staircases. A great hall and a minstrel's gallery provided the final touch of medieval charm.

The only concession to economy was to use the original foundations, and the Messels were delighted when the builders uncovered some genuinely medieval stonework; this was supplemented with historic features sourced from antique shops and dealers. Constrained as she was by the post-war shortage of materials and labour, it took five years for Maud's dream to be realized. But when complete it received the ultimate endorsement: an article by Christopher

Hussey in that bastion of British middle-class taste, *Country Life* magazine.

The family lost much of its personal fortune during the war because Ludwig had unwisely kept it invested in Germany and Russia, but during the post-war reconstruction the Messels soon recovered their wealth. Those whose fortune was based in stocks flourished during the interwar period – unlike the aristocracy, which for decades had suffered from plummeting agricultural returns, steadily rising taxes and massive increases in death duties. Leonard had never been particularly interested in finance and, like his father before him, turned increasingly to horticulture to occupy his later years. He forged a firm friendship with Comber, one that was much more amiable than the distant, but respectful relationship that had earlier existed between his father and the head gardener.

A canny collector of art, Leonard turned his connoisseur's vision on to the gardens. In contrast to his father's promiscuous enthusiasm, his was a more focused approach. He concentrated on rhododendrons, building up the collection of hybrids and cultivars for which Nymans became famous. He was also interested in camellias, and planted masses of hydrangeas to ensure autumn interest. Leonard's passion for collecting also found an outlet in old garden books. By the end of the 1920s Nymans held the best private horticultural library in England, surpassed only by those of the Royal Horticultural Society and the British Museum. The earliest books in the collection, dating from the fifteenth century, would have been written in Latin and bound in leather. Leonard also had German, French and Flemish publications, as well as an unparalleled collection of early English herbals.

Meanwhile, the next generation of children was growing up. In 1920 Leonard and Maud's eldest son, Linley, joined the family stockbroking firm of L. Messel & Co. Their youngest son, Oliver, who resisted pressure to go to university, in 1923

Left above: This temple-like summer house is one of the features designed for the garden in the early twentieth century by Alfred Messel, Ludwig's architect brother. It lies north of the house, on the edge of the Pinetum.

Below left and far left: Roses have always been part of Nymans' charm. Early on, Ludwig Messel and James Comber created a Rose Garden. Of the next generation, it was Maud who delighted in old English roses. Although she was never an active gardener, under her guidance the Top Garden was filled with roses, picturesquely placed around an ancient well.

Right: Leonard and Maud's three children: Oliver (1904–1978), Anne (1902–1992) and Linley (1899–1971). While Linley fulfilled his father's hopes and joined the family stockbroking firm, Oliver turned his back on finance to become a highly successful set designer. Anne grew up to be a celebrated beauty who kept the gossip columnists busy.

enrolled instead in the Slade School of Fine Art – and went on to become one of England's most fashionable set designers. Their only daughter, Anne, having been presented at court, spent the next three years in a debutante swirl. In 1925 she married the extremely eligible young barrister Ronald Armstrong-Jones. The marriage produced two children, Susan and Antony, while Anne became the centre of a busy social circle. In gratitude to her parents for her magnificent wedding and their gift of a house in London's Eaton Square, Anne purchased for them a piece of neglected land just across the road from the main entrance to Nymans.

Through the 1920s and 1930s, new gardening friends signed the guest book, including Frederick Stern, who was developing a glorious garden in a chalk pit at his house, Highdown, near Worthing. Lionel de Rothschild was another; he purchased the 80-hectare/ 200-acre estate of Exbury in Hampshire in 1919 and set about creating what many consider the best woodland garden in England. Among other visitors were: Robert James from Yorkshire, immortalized in the rambling rose named after him, *Rosa* 'Bobbie James'; the eccentric Edward James of West Dean; E.A. Bowles from Myddelton House; Reginald Cory of Dyffryn Gardens; the garden designer Norah Lindsay; and the rosarian Graham Stuart Thomas.

Unlike his father, Leonard took an active role in the Royal Horticultural Society. In 1923, when he exhibited at an RHS flower show for the first time, his rhododendron seedlings came home with a silver medal – and many more awards were to follow. By 1924 Leonard had begun serving as a judge at flower shows and in 1936 he was elected to the

Many good garden plants were named at Nymans. Some resulted from deliberate crosses, while others were discovered as chance seedlings or sports that differed in some interesting way from the usual form. Left: *Magnolia* x *loebneri* 'Leonard Messel', illustrated here with a sprig of forsythia, flowers in early spring. It originated at Nymans in 1955. Above left: Double-flowered *Camellia* 'Maud Messel' was raised by Leonard Messel and named in honour of his wife in 1969. Above centre: *Forsythia suspensa* 'Nymans', introduced in 1954, has bronze-purple stems and, in late winter, primrose-yellow flowers. Above right: *Eucryphia* x *nymansensis*, an evergreen tree with an upright habit and abundant late-summer flowers, was one of Nymans' first introductions. It was spotted in a batch of young plants during the First World War and planted in the Wall Garden.

society's council. The following year James Comber received the Victoria Medal of Honour, the highest accolade the RHS can bestow. (He was also among the first Associates of Honour, an award founded by the society in 1930 to recognize distinguished careers in horticulture.)

As a proud and skilful gardener, Comber's contributions to horticulture were manifold. He had been exhibiting plants ever since his youthful collections of verbena and hardy ferns began winning prizes at local shows. Over the years he became adept at hybridizing rhododendrons and creating new cultivars, many of which were named in honour of the Messel family, including *Magnolia* x *loebneri* 'Leonard Messel' with delicate, starlike, lilac-pink flowers; the pretty pink *Camellia* 'Maud Messel'; *Forsythia suspensa* 'Nymans' with unusual bronze stems; and the much-loved *Eucryphia* x *nymansensis*, a lovely white-flowering summer shrub. In his early twenties Comber had begun contributing articles to the *Gardeners' Chronicle* and other journals. He was frequently asked to judge at garden shows in London and around the country, and was a member of the RHS Rhododendron, Lily and Floral Committees. Meanwhile Comber's eldest child Harold, who had been born, raised and trained at Nymans, was making a name for himself as a horticulturist and plant hunter.

HAROLD COMBER: A DISTINGUISHED FAMILY OF GARDENERS

Harold Frederick Comber (1897–1969) represents the second in three generations of Combers who excelled in horticulture. He was born at Nymans, where his father was head gardener for more than fifty years, and went on to become a gardener, plant collector and lily expert. He began his career at Henry Elwes' garden at Colesbourne Park, Gloucestershire. When the First World War began, and he was exempted from active service because of a knee injury, he suddenly became responsible for the glasshouses and botanical collection as older staff went to war. After the war, he studied at the Royal Botanic Garden Edinburgh, where he excelled, and was sponsored to go plant hunting in the Andes in 1926 and 1927 (where he collected *Azara lanceolata*, seen right). Exploring the terrain with only a child as guide, Comber sent back seeds and herbarium specimens of over 1,200 species. In 1930 he made a further expedition, to Tasmania, where he collected seeds of 147 plants for a syndicate of Lionel de Rothschild's. In 1952 he became lily hybridizer for Jan de Graaff's Oregon Bulb Farm in America, where he published many articles, reared new lily strains and improved production. In 1965 he undertook his final plant-hunting expedition, collecting orchids on the island of Borneo with his son James Comber (1929–2005), a specialist on Indonesian orchids affiliated to the Royal Botanic Gardens, Kew.

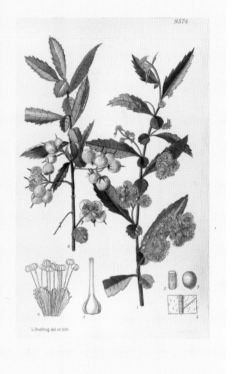

The land that Anne had purchased opposite the main entrance came to be known as 'Tasmania' in the 1930s, when it was used to cultivate Harold Comber's Antipodean and Andean plants.

A society belle, Anne had been one of the fast, decadent, bohemian, bright young things of the 1930s. It came as little surprise when her marriage failed. She was granted a divorce in 1935 and three weeks later married an Irish aristocrat of ancient lineage, Michael Parsons, 6th Earl of Rosse. He came with a 400-hectare/1000-acre estate in County Offaly that included the town of Rosse and the crumbling castle of Birr – which Anne, now Countess of Rosse, set about restoring. The grounds had been landscaped in the late eighteenth century with winding paths, picturesque groves and a lake to reflect the Gothic castle. Famous for the 1.8-metre/6-foot reflecting telescope which had been built in the 1840s by the third earl, the grounds also contained 48 hectares/120 acres of gardens, including a Walled Garden with 300-year-old box hedges.

Anne created a Hornbeam Walk around the old formal garden, which she replanted in seventeenth-century style

Above: *Azara lanceolata* illustrated in *Curtis's Botanical Magazine*. This evergreen shrub with scented flowers was among the herbarium specimens collected by Charles Darwin in Chile in 1834, during his voyage aboard HMS *Beagle*. It was introduced to England in 1927 by Harold Comber, son of Nymans' head gardener, and won an Award of Merit at the RHS Chelsea Flower Show in 1931.
Right top: Oliver and Anne Messel posing in fancy dress. Wilful Anne found Oliver's hedonistic friends from the world of theatre more congenial than the bourgeois company kept by her first husband, the distinguished, ambitious, hard-working lawyer, Ronald Armstrong-Jones.
Right below: Birr Castle, in Ireland, was the family seat of Anne's second husband, Michael Parsons, 6th Earl of Rosse, who had been a contemporary of her brother Oliver's at Eton. Parsons' ancient Irish title and grand estate appealed to her sense of drama and romance. The couple had two sons, half-brothers to the son and daughter Anne had by her first marriage.

with gravel walks, clipped box, urns, statues and billowing beds of lilacs and roses. In one of the courtyards she added a spectacular wisteria pergola and a collection of old roses, no doubt inspired by those at Nymans. She also established herbaceous plants along the Moat Walk and underplanted the ancient forests with flowering shrubs and rhododendrons. The 5th Earl of Rosse had subscribed to two of Ernest Henry Wilson's expeditions to China, a tradition continued by the 6th Earl and Countess of Rosse through their introduction of rarities and support for plant hunters. Birr became the first garden in Ireland to receive a *Metasequoia glyptostroboides* (dawn redwood) after its discovery in China in 1945.

The Rosses spent much time at Nymans and both gardens benefited from the exchange of ideas, advice and material. Following their parents' divorce, Susan and Tony Armstrong-Jones also spent much of their spare time with their Messel grandparents, and for all of them Nymans became the stable hub of their hectic lives. The Rosses, with their intense interest in restoring and preserving old buildings, became founder members of the Georgian Group, created in 1937 to halt the large-scale destruction of Georgian London. Two decades later, in the post-war frenzy of modernization, Anne also founded the Victorian Society to preserve what was left of that eminent heritage.

By the time the Second World War loomed, the Messels had few remaining ties with Germany. However, Leonard did have a cousin living there, the daughter of his uncle Alfred, who had died in 1909. When it became clear that Alfred's reputation as a highly respected architect would no longer protect her from Hitler's anti-Jewish policies, Leonard helped her escape to England. During the war itself Nymans suffered in the same way as many rural estates did: the garden staff was reduced to three old men as the younger ones went off to fight. Many irreplaceable plants in 'Tasmania' died through neglect, and the exotics suffered because there was no fuel allowance for the hothouses. With the aid of two Land Army girls, much of the ornamental gardens were turned over to fruit and vegetables. The shortage of building material, which continued after the war, meant no repairs could be made, and this affected the fragile glasshouses and garden buildings particularly badly.

Above: One night during the brutally cold winter of 1947, the house at Nymans burnt to the ground. Even though more than seventy firemen battled the blaze, the standpipes were frozen so water had to be pumped from a distant pond. The next morning a salvage party was organized, but little of value remained.

The winter of 1946 was notoriously bitter. That the Messels frequently had to resort to blowtorches to warm the frozen pipes was probably a factor in the terrible event that occurred one night in February 1947: the house caught fire and burnt to the ground. Firemen were unable to fight the blaze because both the standpipes and the ladders' iron runners were frozen. Leonard Messel's precious library of rare botanical books was lost, as were the furniture, art and personal effects carefully collected over two generations. Nobody, however, died in the fire.

Unable even to consider rebuilding in that era of post-war shortages, the Messels moved into Holmsted Manor, just a few miles away, and continued to maintain the grounds from a distance. Ironically, the gardens at Nymans were almost enhanced by the dramatic ruin at their heart. As roses tumbled over the Gothic arched doorways and clung to the jagged stone tracery of the windows, as the camellias expanded into open glades and herbaceous borders billowed over paths, Nymans became even more romantic – a sleeping beauty waiting for some prince to wake her. Since the garden

OLIVER MESSEL: DESIGNER FOR THE STAGE

Oliver Hilary Sambourne Messel (1904–1978) was one of the wittiest, most imaginative and sophisticated designers of the twentieth century. He was a pre-eminent figure for many years, creating designs for theatre, ballet, cinema, costumes, furniture, stage sets and interiors. His career began when masks he had designed were used in a production by Serge Diaghilev, founder of the Ballets Russes. He moved on to New York's Broadway where he won a Tony Award for his work on the musical *House of Flowers* (1954), and was nominated for *Rashomon* (1959) and *Gigi* (1973); he was also nominated for an Academy Award as production designer on *Suddenly Last Summer* (1959). During the Second World War, Messel's anarchic talents were put to good use in his role as camouflage officer, when he was responsible for disguising pillboxes as faux haystacks, sham ruins and roadside cafes. After his nephew, Antony Armstrong-Jones, married HRH Princess Margaret, Messel designed Princess Margaret's home on the island of Mustique in the West Indies. By the 1960s his exquisite taste and dazzling opulence was at odds with the prevailing kitchen-sink aesthetic. Stimulated by the vibrancy of the Caribbean, he bought a house in Barbados and began a new career designing glamorous, fantastical houses for wealthy retirees.

was essentially informal, it was not as difficult to maintain as other gardens of equal size. Even so, the future of Nymans weighed heavily on Leonard and Maud, particularly as they grew increasingly old and infirm. Their eldest son, Linley, having moved to America, severed contact with the family. Anne already had too much property to oversee; and Oliver, a designer with an international clientele, was deeply attached to Nymans but had little interest in taking over the family estate. Throughout his life he kept a cottage in the grounds and many of his most famous designs clearly owe much to the romantic, opulent sophistication of the garden at Nymans. Particularly notable are the designs he created for George Cukor's 1936 film *Romeo and Juliet*, with its garland-draped balcony suspended from high, arched walls, and the Royal Opera House's 1946 production of *The Sleeping Beauty* with its enchanting garden scenes.

In 1947 the Royal Horticultural Society, responding to its members' post-war troubles, approached the National Trust with a proposal that it should add gardens 'of outstanding beauty, design or historic interest' to its portfolio of land and houses of national importance. In 1948 Lawrence Johnston's

Hidcote Manor became the first garden accepted under the new scheme. Soon after, Leonard Messel entered into negotiations with the Trust about Nymans.

In 1953, just before his eighty-first birthday, Leonard Messel died. Three months later James Comber also died, signalling the end of another era at Nymans. The National Trust took Nymans under its wing with an endowment of £20,000, and in 1954 the property opened to the public. Anne, following her husband's death, moved into a renovated section of the house, took over as director of the garden, and oversaw the post-war renovations carried out by the new head gardener, Cecil Nice. Decades of unchecked growth were taken in hand, and glades cut through the Pinetum. The grounds were planted for year-round interest, with the addition of low-maintenance ground cover where possible. Eventually a guidebook was published to encourage visitors, and the garden adapted to receive them in greater numbers.

In 1960 Maud Messel died; several months later her grandson, Antony Armstrong-Jones, married HRH Princess Margaret, stimulating public interest in the Messels and Nymans. In the great storm of October 1987, nearly 500

Right: Despite its ancient appearance, the dovecote dates from the 1920s reconstruction of the house. While the rooftop lantern held doves, the body of the building was used as a garden room and art studio. The dovecote's presence in the courtyard added the medieval air that Maud Messel strived to create, with its echoes of a feudal privilege that originated in the twelfth century.

FOUNDATION OF THE NATIONAL TRUST

The National Trust was created in 1895 'to preserve places of historic interest or natural beauty'. Its founders, the housing reformer Octavia Hill, the clergyman Hardwicke Rawnsley and a solicitor for the Commons Preservation Society, Sir Robert Hunter, shared a zeal for social reform and a love of nature. Initially, the trust focused on modest properties, and few could have predicted that it would be the salvation of Britain's great country estates. The first property the trust acquired was a hilltop which provided 'open-air sitting rooms for the poor'. This was followed by: a medieval clergy house in Alfriston; Tintagel's fourteenth-century post office; some shoreline in the Lake District; and a fragment of East Anglian fenland. The first purchase of a grand house, the Tudor manor of Barrington Court, in Somerset, caused great controversy because of the high cost of repairs and maintenance. Thereafter the trust became more careful about which properties it accepted, often requiring these to come with an endowment or have potential to generate significant income. The National Trust Act of 1937 supported the trust's new direction by allowing that any house bequeathed to the National Trust would be exempt from death duties; and under the Country House Scheme the donor's family could continue to live on the site for another two generations. As death duties had risen steadily through the late nineteenth and early twentieth centuries, many owners of country estates, unable to find the staff or finance the maintenance required, simply blew up their houses and sold off the land for development. By 1955, five country houses per week were being demolished. In that time of post-war austerity, when food was still being rationed, building material was restricted and socialism was in vogue, there was little sentiment for these emblems of privilege. The National Trust stepped in to save many important houses – and later, gardens – to preserve them as part of Britain's cultural heritage.

trees were lost from the grounds, but the carnage fortuitously opened up views that had been hidden for half a century. Although the rhododendrons were damaged, new shoots grew up from the stumps. Long-lost flowers suddenly sprouted in areas that had been shrouded in shade for decades. A temperate winter following the storm ensured that the new, young plants were not struck down, and the garden emerged more beautiful than ever.

After Anne died in 1992, her living quarters were restored and opened to the public. It was a development much appreciated by visitors. With its low ceilings and leaded glass windows, its quirky rooms stuffed with paintings, books and photographs, its antique rugs, embroidered tapestries and polished furniture, this surviving part of the house completes the rich, vibrant picture of a bohemian retreat, whose fortunes, to a large extent, mirrored those of the country at large.

Left: The long curve of the Lime Avenue links the lower part of the Pinetum to the pleasure grounds around the house. The tree trunks frame views across the valley, and wild flowers fill the meadow in the style promoted by William Robinson.
Above: Hurricane-force winds felled at least 500 trees at Nymans during the great storm of October 1987, including the huge, old monkey puzzle tree and deodar cedar on the front lawn. The pergola, wreathed in ancient wisteria, was also flattened, as was the shelter belt of yew, larch and laurel.
Below right: The Garden Room, with its cosy sofas, cushions, tapestries and throws, is different to the Tudor-revival decor of the house in the 1930s, when beamed ceilings and heavy, Jacobean furniture were the height of fashion.

HIDCOTE MANOR GARDEN

One of the most influential of English gardens was created by the eccentric Major Lawrence Johnston. In 1907 Johnston's American mother purchased a seventeenth-century farmhouse on a bleak, exposed hill in Gloucestershire, intending to transform her reclusive son into an English gentleman-farmer. Instead, Johnston took to gardening. He created an elegant Arts and Crafts-style garden, consisting of twenty-eight separate rooms, each enclosed in stone walls or in high beech, box and yew

hedging. Linked by walks and vistas, each space is furnished differently with pools, fountains, topiary, elegant flower beds and simple orchards. Although there is no overall plan and the garden is unrelated to the house, its clean architectural lines, range of plants and variety of different moods have inspired modernists and romantics alike. A keen plantsman, Johnston took part in one plant-hunting expedition and helped to finance several others, and by the 1920s he had twelve full-time gardeners working at Hidcote. In 1924 Johnston purchased Serre de la Madone, an estate in the south of France where he went to escape the bitter English winters. He proceeded to create a Mediterranean garden on the steep, olive-terraced slopes, filling the space with colourful exotics. In 1948, having no family and no heirs, Johnston donated Hidcote to the National Trust and retired permanently to Serre de la Madone.

SISSINGHURST CASTLE

One of England's best-loved gardens, Sissinghurst is famous as much for its unorthodox owners as for its elegant collection of garden rooms. In 1930 the novelist Vita Sackville-West and her diplomat husband Harold Nicolson purchased the ruins of a grand Elizabethan castle in Kent. Reprising the classic gender balance, he devised a formal layout linking the various walks, walls and enclosures, which she softened with abundant, exuberant, extravagant planting. Over the years, they created a series of garden rooms

Left top: A strong architectural sensibility underpins the gardens at Hidcote. High hedges, clipped topiary, neatly trimmed lawns, richly planted beds, pleached allées and grassy paths link the many enclosures.

Left below: The estate that Vita Sackville-West and her husband purchased in 1930 sits on an ancient site ('hurst' being the Saxon word for an enclosed wood). The brick gatehouse with its lookout tower was constructed in the sixteenth century by one of Henry VIII's privy councillors. It was here, in her study high over the gardens, that Vita would entertain lovers of both sexes – when not occupied with writing poetry, books and garden articles. In 1938 the garden was opened to the public with an entrance fee of one shilling, leading Vita to refer to her garden visitors as 'shillingses'.

Below: While its walled garden and hedged enclosures provide an illusion of privacy, one of the most magnificent features of Polesden Lacey is the view from the terrace, outwards over the rolling Surrey hills.

around the central brick entrance tower where Vita wrote and entertained her many lovers. From 1946, when she became gardening correspondent for the *Observer*, a wider public became intimate with Vita's horticultural triumphs and tragedies, her passions, obsessions and infatuations, as she emoted over her famous White Garden, Persian-inspired Nut Walk, Cottage Garden, and all the other lawns, walks and garden spaces within the castle moat. In spite of serving as a founder member on the National Trust's garden committee, Vita dreaded the prospect of her beloved creation ending in the trust's cold, corporate grip. Nonetheless, in 1967, five years after her death, her husband handed Sissinghurst over to the National Trust, where it remains one of the most popular gardens in their care.

POLESDEN LACEY

A classic Edwardian country estate, Polesden Lacey was remodelled in the early years of the twentieth century by the Honourable Mrs Ronald Greville. Known as a 'collector of Kings', Greville was the illegitimate daughter of a brewery multimillionaire and a former boarding-house keeper. Her rise to prominence indicates just how permeable Edwardian society had become. The villa sits in the midst of an extensive, eighteenth-century landscaped park; its long, grass walk dates from the seventeenth century. Greville, however, drew on the Arts and Crafts style when she transformed the large walled kitchen garden into varied pleasure grounds, with a series of hedged enclosures, billowing herbaceous borders, a Rock Garden, croquet lawn, Winter Garden and Dog Cemetery. In the Rose Garden, the highlight of the pleasure grounds, is a central avenue straddled by climbing roses supported on arches. Greville obligingly remodelled a whole wing of the house to ensure that Edward VII could entertain his mistress in comfort. She was also canny enough to cultivate his morose daughter-in-law Mary, to make sure that, when Edward died, the royal visits would continue. The future King George VI and his bride Elizabeth Bowes-Lyon honeymooned at Polesden Lacey and, although Greville promised to leave the estate to them, she bequeathed it instead to the National Trust. However, she did leave her magnificent collection of jewels to Queen Elizabeth.

GREAT DIXTER

GREAT DIXTER

CHRISTOPHER LLOYD'S PROVOCATIVE PARADISE

The twentieth century was a volatile time for England's gardens and gardeners. Two world wars, the loss of armies of gardening staff and the break-up of great estates resulted in the decline of many grand gardens. While the escape to suburbia, with its well-groomed front gardens, brought horticulture to the masses, the rise of gardening magazines engendered a restless search for the new and different. As garden lovers adjusted to increasingly small plots, the emphasis gravitated from design to plants and the century consequently saw a rise in amateur plantsmen and plantswomen. During the first half of the century, formality dominated, as Arts and Crafts historicism vied with abstract modernism in the field of landscape architecture. Latterly, the growing awareness of climate change and diminishing natural resources has led to the search for a more ecological and sustainable approach, creating an interest in naturalistic perennial, meadow and prairie planting. The most provocative and influential garden of recent times, a garden that anticipated many of these trends, is Great Dixter.

A great Janus of a place, Dixter has its roots firmly in the past and its crown defiantly in the future. Like many great gardens, it reflects the work of several strong personalities and several generations of obsessive gardeners. Dixter today is associated with the incorrigible Christopher Lloyd, the much-loved, much-indulged *enfant terrible* of British horticulture. Christo, as he was known to many, was born at Dixter in 1921 and died there eighty-five years later. But the garden itself was in fact created by his parents, with the help of the great Edwardian architect Edwin Lutyens. It was they who laid down the bones of the place, which Christo went on to embellish with his distinctive, vibrant planting.

Right: The long grass of the Orchard sweeps right up to the garden, with only the flagstone path and adjacent strip of mown grass separating the artifice of the Long Border from the wildflower meadow beyond.
Below: Christo loved his short-haired dachshunds. He owned several over the years and named all of them after plants: Tulipa, Dahlia, Canna, Crocus and Yucca.

If Nymans was built on faux medievalism
(pages 161–3), Dixter was authentically of the
Middle Ages. Its landscape still bears the marks
of medieval ridge-and-furrow ploughing,
while at the heart of the garden is the mid-
fifteenth century manor house which gives
the estate its name. In 1910 Nathaniel and
Daisy Lloyd purchased the 180-hectare/450-
acre estate, with its crumbling timber-frame
house, near Northiam in East Sussex. As the
property had been on the market for a decade,
it took both courage and imagination to see
its possibilities. The house sat on an exposed
ridge facing south-west, with magnificent
views towards the wet meadows of the
Rother Valley and Bodiam Castle, and the
sea, not quite visible, just 16 kilometres/10
miles away. As there is little stone suitable
for building in the chalk and sandy loam of
south-east England, most ancient houses in
the area were constructed of oak, felled from
the forest that once covered the Weald. By
the early twentieth century, most of this
forest had disappeared and one of the first tasks at Dixter
was to plant a shelter belt of ash trees to the west, to
shield the garden from the wind. This cut out much of
the view, encouraging an insular, inward-looking approach
that contributed to the garden's intimate atmosphere.

Daisy Lloyd was a formidable woman. Known to her
family as 'the management', she cultivated her six children
with the same obsessive zeal as she cultivated her garden.
Nathaniel was a more distant figure; a successful businessman
who pioneered colour printing, he retired at the age of forty-
one and moved his young wife to the country to raise their
children while he pursued interests in golf, photography
and architecture. Nathaniel went on to study architecture,
and he wrote two books on the subject: *A History of English
Brickwork* in 1925 and *A History of the English House* in 1931.

Although originally he intended to restore the house
alone, Nathaniel soon realized he would need professional
help. Having rejected the plans of the venerable firm of
Ernest George & Yeates, he turned to England's most
eligible architect, Sir Edwin Lutyens, who was then
at the height of his career. Lutyens had first come to
prominence by building comfortable weekend houses for

sophisticated urbanites moving to the Home Counties. While still sympathetic to vernacular materials and techniques, by 1910 Lutyens had begun to experiment with the minimalism and monumentality that were to characterize his later style. At Dixter he was able to apply both his early Arts and Crafts sensibilities and his growing taste for simplicity. Although Lutyens often worked with the garden designer Gertrude Jekyll, she had no direct involvement here.

When the Lloyds first purchased Dixter, the derelict farm contained assorted barns and outbuildings, a few ponds, two orchards with some picturesque old trees and a lot of nettles. The medieval house would originally have consisted of an open hall with a central hearth, in which shared space the servants and family would live, sleep and eat. The master would preside from a dais at one end of the hall while the kitchen activities would take place at the other. In the late fifteenth century, a time of growing concern for personal privacy and the hierarchical division of space, a solar was created at Dixter. This was a raised room reserved for the master's family, allowing them to withdraw from the noise, smell and bustle of the great hall and pursue solitary activities such as embroidery, reading and writing. As such activities required good light, solars were generally built facing south to take advantage of the sun. Further changes were made in Tudor times: two storeys were inserted within the hall and a large chimney added. Over the centuries new windows and doors were incorporated, and spaces were further subdivided; but when the Lloyds purchased the house in 1910 its original lines were still very much evident.

Under Lutyens' direction, and with Nathaniel overseeing the works, Dixter was stripped of later accretions to reveal the great hall open to the ceiling. In a nearby village Lutyens found a derelict sixteenth-century yeoman's hall, roofed with tin and used as a cattle shelter. Nathaniel purchased it for its scrap value; the timbers were numbered and dismantled before being transported the 14 kilometres/9 miles to Great Dixter. Here the house was reassembled to create a master bedroom, which was immediately filled with an enormous oak bed, copied from a grand, Italian Renaissance original. Lutyens then constructed a service wing to link the two halls. While Lutyens' wing employed the same bricks and tiles,

Above: Even though Gertrude Jekyll did not design the gardens at Dixter, her influence infuses the place. Perhaps this is because of Daisy's visits to Jekyll's nursery to buy plants. On one such occasion, Jekyll gave Christo her blessing, hoping that he would grow up to become a great gardener.
Opposite, top left: The sparsely furnished great hall was used as the family's living and dining room. In addition to antique, high-backed chairs and a refectory table in oak, there was a second table made by Nathaniel and his son Patrick in 1932.
Opposite, top right: Nathaniel Lloyd was so enamoured of early English architecture that he trained himself in architectural drawing and, having retired at the age of forty-one, established a small practice. He wrote frequently on the subject and published two historical monographs.
Opposite below: This is the crumbling yeoman's hall that Nathaniel purchased in the nearby village of Benenden and had transported piece by piece, in order to create a new wing at Great Dixter.

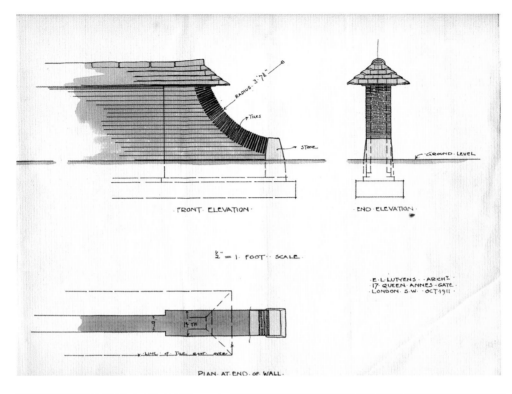

·FRONT·ELEVATION·

·END·ELEVATION·

$\frac{1}{2}" = 1·FOOT··SCALE·$

·E·L·LUTYENS··ARCHT·
17·QUEEN·ANNES·GATE·
LONDON·S.W·OCT·1911·

·PLAN·AT·END·OF·WALL·

TUDOR REVIVAL: AN IDEALIZED VIEW OF THE PAST

The Tudor revival reached its apex in the 1920s when, still shocked by the carnage of the recent war, the nation sought refuge in the romantic vision of a past era. Harking back to a time when England's influence was at its height, tastemakers idealized all things Tudor. When Liberty rebuilt their London shop in 1924, they chose the distinctively mock-Tudor black-and-white, half-timbered style to reflect their establishment values. Many in the country-house brigade bought up neglected medieval manor houses, which they renovated and adapted with modern conveniences. Others built new houses incorporating old materials or artificially aged new building materials, to make the beams seem gnarled and to promote lichen on the tiles. Lower down the social scale, Tudor-style houses proliferated in the new middle-class suburbs, and Tudor-revival was also the preferred style for public housing developments. The prevailing nostalgia sparked renewed interest

The South Hall at Great Dixter

in handicrafts such as tapestry, embroidery and woodworking, and engendered a fascination for peasant culture, inspiring Vaughan Williams to record folk songs and Cecil Sharp to document country dances.

Left: Nathaniel planned to restore Dixter himself, but soon found he needed expert help. He approached Sir Edwin Lutyens, who was then at the height of his career. Lutyens' intricate plan for one section of the garden wall (left above) and the finished structure (left below) demonstrate his characteristic use of tiles laid on end for decorative effect.

steep roof and leaded windows as the medieval buildings, it was unashamedly contemporary. This new space was to house the offices, kitchen, pantries and servants' quarters for six indoor staff, with bedrooms and bathrooms on two floors above – maids being relegated to the small rooms at the top.

In August 1911, with work on the house well under way, Lutyens presented his plan for the garden. Cleverly integrating the outbuildings, he created a patchwork of walls, steps and paths extending outwards from the house. The resulting series of enclosures makes the modest 2.5-hectare/ 6-acre garden feel much larger than it really is. The cowshed had its crumbling walls removed and was reinvented as an open loggia, with beds of sweet-smelling annuals planted in front. The roof of the chicken house was raised on tile columns, providing a second loggia. An existing 'Brunswick' fig was planted against the old barn, where its leaves stood out against the weathered boards. Four raised, brick water troughs were redeployed as ornamental pools. The medieval barn, nineteenth-century oast house and thatched stable (the decrepit roof of which the Lloyds replaced with shingle) were used to define the boundaries of the Barn Garden.

Lutyens' appreciation of vernacular detail is evident throughout the garden, in such features as the brick walls, the

GREAT DIXTER. THE TERRACE STEPS. 6022.

tiled coping, the arched doorways picked out with tiles laid on end, and the semicircular steps leading down to the Sunk Garden. Although his plan employed straight lines, it was neither symmetrical nor formal: the enclosures are suggested rather than defined, and each of the many spaces has a distinctly different mood and scale. The main entrance leads through the Front Meadow up to the ancient front porch. At the back of the house three paths fan out in a *patte d'oie*, the central one extending to the Lower Moat, and the outer two leading into the Orchard and to what was originally the Rose Garden. The rest of the garden is linked by a circuit walk, a wide stone path circumnavigating the house and connecting the High Garden (where fruit and vegetables were originally grown) with the Barn Garden and adjacent Wall Garden on the opposite boundary. A square, flagstone terrace was placed up against the house, beneath which a second, narrower terrace extends at right angles into the Long Border.

The major expenses of the garden were the box and yew hedges, and the stone for the paths – much of which was reclaimed London paving and provided a suitably aged appearance. While Lutyens laid out the walks, designed the garden walls and suggested green enclosures, Nathaniel

Above: Lutyens' design for the garden included a layout of paths radiating out through the Orchard from an intricate circular pattern of steps, set between the Lower Terrace and the Long Border.

Above: Elements of the pre-existing farmyard were incorporated into the design of the Rose Garden: the old cow byre, known as the 'hovel', was transformed into a picturesque loggia and the circular, brick water trough became a decorative pool. Years later, the roses were removed by Christo to create his controversial Exotic Garden.

Following pages: Old English architecture being Nathaniel Lloyd's passion, he ensured that the medieval manor house was at the heart of the garden, its warm, red brick and ochre plaster providing a dramatic backdrop to Dixter's many garden spaces.

oversaw the hedges, supervising the planting, maintenance and trimming of the many yards of yew and box. Nathaniel also adapted Lutyens' plan, replacing a number of his proposed walls with hedging, which he thought was more appropriate to the ancient house. He also rejected the formal path that Lutyens wanted to drive through the Orchard, adding instead a wheelbarrow path in brick. Planting soon softened Lutyens' design, as the stonework became studded with self-sown valerian and erigeron. The Lloyds chose hydrangeas and other billowing shrubs to flank paths and mark steps. Peach and apricot trees were planted against the warm walls of the house, and a magnolia placed beside the double staircase descending from the terrace.

Near the Rose Garden, set into a deep hedge, was a massive oak bench known as the 'family pew'. It overlooked a flat expanse of lawn where Nathaniel practised his golf – and continued doing so even after he had filled the space with tall topiary figures resembling giant chess pieces. As he became more adventurous, he turned the lavender-lined approach to the High Garden into a green aviary with different topiary birds: nightingales, blackbirds, pheasants, fighting cocks. Over time the birds began to resemble each other, so they

Above: The peacock topiary at Dixter, which at first glance might look like interwar whimsy, is in fact almost modernist in its abstract simplicity.

were all clipped into simple, peacock-like forms perched on large pyramidal plinths. Nathaniel also created other, more architectural features, clipping huge yew trees into archways and shaping the tops of hedges into castellations.

Nathaniel became so skilled at topiary that he wrote a book on the subject, *Garden Craftsmanship in Yew and Box* (1925). The garden soon became famous for its abstract clipped forms and high, architectural hedges, provoking William Robinson – who hated the artifice of the practice – to make a snide reference to the topiary at Dixter in later editions of *The English Flower Garden*.

Another of Nathaniel's important contributions at Dixter was the Sunk Garden, which he created in 1923 in the centre of the Barn Garden. Lutyens had intended this area to be a croquet lawn, but Nathaniel wanted something more ornamental and, while he held with William Robinson's dislike of statuary and fountains, he did feel the need for some sort of water feature in the garden. His opportunity came in the wake of the First World War, when the great hall had been used as a convalescent hospital and the Barn Garden turned

LIVING SCULPTURE: THE FASHION FOR TRAINING AND PRUNING

The practice of clipping evergreen plants into figurative shapes has flourished since Roman times. The word 'topiary' derives from the Latin *topiarius*, meaning an ornamental gardener – a creator of *topia* or 'places'. Pliny the Elder in his *Natural History* (*c.*AD77) celebrated this form of living sculpture, describing cypresses clipped into all sorts of wonderful tableaux including hunting scenes and fleets of ships. The art of topiary survived into the Middle Ages, as is shown by the small trees clipped into tiers that often figure in illuminated manuscripts. The practice was popular in the Renaissance, when the fascination with geometry was expressed in formal green spheres, cubes, obelisks and pyramids. In the baroque period, topiary was often used architecturally to create allées, living walls and green theatres. Topiary fell from favour in the eighteenth century, with the move towards natural parkland, but the twentieth-century revival of historical styles, along with the interwar penchant for whimsy, restored its popularity. While box and yew are most commonly used, many other woody evergreens with small leaves and dense foliage make good topiary subjects – including osmanthus, holly, shrub honeysuckle (*Lonicera nitida*) and privet.

Above: Hedge trimmers were introduced at Great Dixter soon after the Second World War. Even so, it usually takes from August to November to work around the garden clipping the eighteen birds and other yew topiary specimens.

over to vegetable production. After the conflict had ended, Nathaniel reclaimed this messy plot and transformed it into a sunken garden with a central octagonal pool surrounded by flagstones, and backed by drystone walls interplanted with alpines. This peaceful space is filled with appropriately cottagey perennials, although Nathaniel punctuated the four corners with *Yucca gloriosa*, whose spear-shaped leaves were echoed by the bearded irises at their bases.

Nathaniel died in 1933. Daisy then took control of the garden and for the next four decades she presided with an iron trowel. She was a passionate plantswoman who taught her children the Latin names of plants and tested them ruthlessly on plant identification. When the boys were away at school she would send them weekly bundles of fresh flowers and frequent letters, in which she often extolled the virtues of the evolving garden. Daisy was catholic in her floral tastes and pioneered many unusual plant combinations. She was perfectly content to mix foreign imports with her

native plants as long as they thrived in the local Sussex soil. William Robinson's *The English Flower Garden* (1883) was her bible, and like Robinson she was more concerned with a plant's requirements than its origins.

Above: The Sunk Garden was added to Lutyens' original plan by Nathaniel Lloyd, who wanted a water feature. The octagonal pool is surrounded by the Barn Garden (left), enclosed on one side by a yew hedge.
Below: Camassia is a North-American perennial from moist meadows. Dixter's naturalistic drifts have been copied widely.

Under Daisy's reign the garden became softer and more natural. Although Christo would later be credited with popularizing the meadow style, it was Daisy who first introduced this approach to Dixter. She had a passion for wild flowers. On her arrival at Dixter she had arranged for the upper moat to be drained, and used the resulting area of damp turf for her first nursery. Here she raised polyanthus, blue *Anemone apennina*, purple *Orchis mascula* and snake's head fritillaries to naturalize in the meadows and lawns. Soon she transformed the rough grass in front of the house into a flowery mead, sprinkled with wild daffodils, crocuses and the spring-flowering plants from her nursery. Native orchids and drifts of the charming, star-flowered camassia followed in summer. Daisy also planted up the land around the Horse Pond, at the entrance to the estate. Originally created for the working of iron ore, when iron manufacture was a thriving local industry, the shallow pond later proved convenient as place for work-weary farm horses to drink and wallow. Since it was no longer needed for this purpose, Daisy transformed the area into a water garden embellished with wild flowers, with added clumps of gorse and heather in honour of Nathaniel's Scottish mother.

Dixter's famous Long Border was originally Daisy's preserve and it was here that she would express her love of labour-intensive annuals. When the garden was first designed, the Lloyds commissioned Sir George Thorold to draw up a planting plan for the border. Clearly much in thrall to Gertrude Jekyll, Thorold punctuated the corners with blocks of Jekyll's favourite *Bergenia cordifolia*. He also followed her tiered planting, creating a back layer of shrubs – tree lupins, guelder roses, cistus, olearia and lilacs – with a lower layer of gladioli, antirrhinums and Canterbury bells. The all-important dahlias were backed by clumps of zebra grass (*Miscanthus sinensis* 'Zebrinus'), as was the fashion at the time. The rest of the border contained perennials, including asters, phlox, kniphofia and helianthemums.

Daisy was never one to opt for low-maintenance plants. In the early years there were nine gardeners to work on the property; but even after the First World War, when the outdoor staff was much reduced, she continued to fill her garden with annuals and biennials. She carefully sowed, pricked out, potted up and planted her colourful salvias and rudbeckias, her scented nicotianas, stocks and mignonette. Bright orange and yellow tithonia, varied asters and spider-like cleomes were grown in readiness for the summer gap when the sweet Williams and foxgloves died back.

One of the first changes Daisy made following the death of her husband was to remove the yuccas from the Sunk Garden. She considered their spike-tipped leaves a danger to her beloved children and replaced them with four *Malus sargentii*, a species of crab apple that she had seen at the RHS Chelsea Flower Show. This spreading, deciduous

Right top: A painfully shy child, Christo was devoted to his mother. It was from her that he acquired his love of gardening.

Right below: In 1930 when he was nine, Christo was sent to board at his prep school, Wellesley House, near Broadstairs on the Kent coast. Although it was only 80 kilometres/50 miles away he and his mother wrote constantly. She addressed him as 'My darling Lambikins' and signed herself 'Mother Sheep Ma-a-a-a'. His letters to her are full of precociously detailed observations on natural history in general and flowers in particular.

Below: A keen photographer, Nathaniel Lloyd carefully documented his family life and the development of the house and gardens at Great Dixter. This picture shows Daisy at one end of the Long Border.

tree provides glorious red berries in autumn, and although the fruit is usually too tart to eat, their high level of pectin was useful in setting the jam that Daisy prepared in great quantities every year.

All Daisy's children were forced to take part in the garden, but Christo was her youngest and most biddable child. As he showed an early enthusiasm for gardening she kept him by her side, teaching him her methods, instilling in him her rituals and routines. With her encouragement Christo began a collection of cacti, which was diligently watered by family and staff while he was away. When Christo was at prep school in Broadstairs, Daisy sent him seeds to plant in his garden patch; when he went on to study modern languages at Cambridge University, she would commandeer him at weekends and in the holidays to help her in the garden. It was Daisy who taught Christo to pick and arrange the great vases of flowers that always filled the rooms at Dixter. It was from her that he learned to value foliage so highly. The South African honey bush (*Melianthus major*), with its massive, silvery pinnate leaves, was one of his favourites, and throughout his life Christo was as happy with a vase of handsome foliage or berried branches as with any grand bouquet. In the winter he would decorate the great hall with large urns of oriental bittersweet (*Celastrus orbiculatus*) combined with wintersweet (*Chimonanthus praecox*) and Chinese witch hazel (*Hamamelis mollis*), whose scents would infuse the room.

Christo had intended to continue his studies with a postgraduate degree in architecture, following in his father's footsteps, but the Second World War intervened. The great hall was turned over to evacuees, the gardens were once again dug up for vegetables, and all the able young men went off to fight. Christo became a gunner in the Royal Artillery and was sent to East Africa where the unexpectedly green landscape of Kenya fascinated him. He spent hours exploring the countryside and each week would send seeds and corms back to his mother, along with vivid descriptions of the brightly coloured plants he saw: dahlias and snapdragons, swathes of

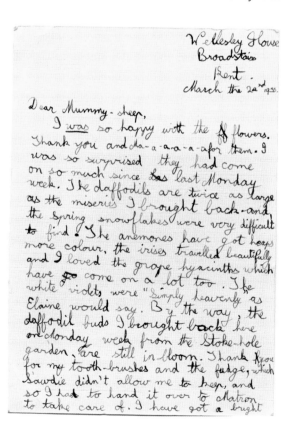

orange and yellow kniphofias. In 1947, on being demobbed, Christo shifted his focus to horticulture and enrolled at Wye College in Kent. As Wye was just 40 kilometres/25 miles from Dixter he could keep an eye on the gardens, rushing back for weekends and even the occasional evening. College gave Christo the practical and scientific training he needed to supplement Daisy's idiosyncratic tuition. It also gave him the authority to challenge her dominance in the garden.

Christo was clearly a diligent student. After graduating he went on to lecture at the college for four years until a contretemps with the management provoked him to resign. In 1954 he returned to Dixter, where he would spend the rest of his life. He and Daisy embarked on a pleasant round of shared activities: needlepoint in the evenings, visiting gardens in the afternoons. They travelled to East Lambrook Manor in Somerset to help Christo's friend Margery Fish weed her cottage beds. They went to Sissinghurst, nearby, where Vita Sackville-West called Christo 'the expert' and Daisy referred to Vita as 'Mrs Nicolson'. They charted the changes being made by Lanning Roper at Scotney Castle, also in Kent, where Christo soon developed a passion for the handsome American designer. Glyndebourne was another place they frequented, since Christo adored opera, and he went on to offer his services as their gardening consultant. Several times a year, even as he became elderly, he would perambulate the grounds with Mary Christie and her head gardener, suggesting improvements before retiring to lunch with the singers and musicians.

But Christo's major preoccupation was always Dixter. By now reduced to a staff of only three gardeners, he and Daisy opened a plant nursery to supplement the diminishing income from Nathaniel's pre-war investments. While catering largely to passing visitors, they also built up a mail-order trade that ultimately accounted for a quarter of the business. Their speciality was clematis, Christo's favourite plant, to which was added a stock of unusual plants. This charmingly amateurish operation was set up beside the garden gate where unlabelled plants with no price attached were sold in little clay pots, the final sum being calculated on a scrap of paper in a dim potting shed. The nursery continues to this day; it is somewhat more professional but has lost none of its charm.

In the late 1950s Christo began writing articles on gardens and plants – a task for which he had been well prepared by the weekly letters he wrote to Daisy from school. (She would correct his grammar and spelling even as she protested her undying love for him and apprised him of the minute changes in their garden.) An indication of Dixter's growing fame came in 1963 when Christo was invited to write a weekly column for *Country Life*, the magazine that had first bestowed the imprimatur of success on the garden by printing an article about it fifty years earlier. In his inimitably engaging

Below: Today the nursery is an important source of income for Dixter. While still small and intimate, it is run along more professional lines than in the early days, when Daisy and Christo sold clematis from the garden gate.

column Christo combined expert horticultural knowledge with dexterous literary skill, discussing his ideas, describing his experiments, deliberating on his own and other peoples' gardens. Over the forty-two years in which he contributed to *Country Life*, he drew in subjects such as poetry, music and pets, being humorously dogmatic, and weaving elaborate conceits while littering the text with snobbish aperçus. And through it all he maintained a delightfully conspiratorial tone, forever exhorting his readers to ignore passing fashion, reject polite gardening and above all, to follow their own fancies. For someone who was so repressed in his own life, Christo clearly found great freedom of expression in his garden. In the late 1970s he began writing monthly for the *Observer Magazine*, and later still became garden correspondent for the *Guardian* newspaper.

Christo's first book, *The Mixed Border*, was published in 1957. His final book, *Exotic Planting for Adventurous Gardeners*, was published several months after his death, in 2007. These titles chart his horticultural odyssey from competent Arts and Crafts gardener to avant-garde trendsetter. In between, a dozen books of varying quality were published – some illustrated with Christo's own rather fuzzy photographs, others professionally illustrated with glorious garden images. While some works were essentially rehashes of his weekly column, others provided new ideas and information. His most popular book, *The Well-Tempered Garden* (1970), takes its title from Bach's collection of preludes and fugues, *The Well-Tempered Clavier*. Later, friends would fondly refer to Lloyd as the 'ill-tempered gardener', alluding to his notorious irascibility especially when confronted with stupid questions or recalcitrant plants. In one of his early columns for *Country Life*, Christo advised his readers: 'if a plant bores you … pull it out', which is rather the attitude he took to people.

With garden fame came horticultural friends and travel overseas. In 1969 Christo went to Kashmir to look at alpines with the designer John Codrington. His first international lecture tour was to Canada and America in 1983. Then in 1989 he joined Beth Chatto on a lecture tour that encompassed New Zealand, Australia and America; and later that year went to Japan with Ken Hadley, a gardener from the Vancouver botanic gardens. In 1993 he went searching

Above: One of Christo's most successful books was *Clematis*, published in 1965 and still a standard reference for gardeners. In his typically intelligent yet accessible style, Christo discusses individual cultivars and advises on practical matters. But he also reveals how he moved on from his first love – glamorous, mauve-flowered *C*. 'W.E. Gladstone' – and came to appreciate even the tiniest, most insignificant flowers within the genus. It is this combination of sensible instruction with outspoken opinion that has delighted readers over the decades.

Above: Contrary to received wisdom on planting design, Christo used tall, airy plants such as teasels at the front of his borders. They act as a veil, coaxing visitors to peer beyond and engage fully with the garden.

Following pages: From early spring all the way into winter, the Long Border is in a constant state of transition: bulbs, perennials, shrubs, trees and climbers form a shifting kaleidoscope of colour, shape and texture. The scene is further enlivened by carefully nurtured annuals and serendipitous self-seeders – important elements in Christo's technique of succession planting.

for tulips in Turkey with garden writer Anna Pavord. All these adventures introduced to Dixter a range of new plants and opportunities for new ways to combine them, particularly in the famous Long Border.

The Long Border was Christo's real trial ground, and as he took over from his mother he began to fill the space with unusual new plants, such as bright yellow, phallic *Arum creticum* – which only flowers for a few days but was deemed worth the space for the excitement it brought. Here he tested hardiness, experimenting with textures, forms and colour combinations. *Lathraea clandestina* (purple toothwort), a parasitic plant, was placed near the *Salix alba* to liven up the border in early spring. Cannas were placed alongside the more traditional buddleias, hypericums, perovskias and caryopteris. In late summer the borders would still be filled with colour, from dahlias, Michaelmas daisies and two purple-flowered hebes, 'Midsummer Beauty' and 'Autumn Glory'. In Lutyens' original design the border had been 40 metres/130 feet long; Christo extended this by a third. He also dug up the strip of grass running alongside it, to increase the depth of planting – making the border a massive 60 metres/200 feet long by 4.5 metres/15 feet deep. Christo filled the back of his enhanced space with small trees, placed flowering shrubs in the middle ground and low edging plants in front. Then he subverted this perfectly choreographed profile by deliberately placing tall, airy plants in front where they would command attention and oblige visitors to peer beyond them in order to see the plants behind. At the far end of the border, backed by a hedge, Christo put one of the simple oak benches designed by Lutyens, its solid lines echoing the oak timbers of the house. Here, at the edge of the garden, he would retire with his evening whisky to contemplate the world.

Christo's main contribution, and one that influenced not only Dixter but horticulture in general, was his idea of succession planting. The Long Border is where he practised this fine art, heroically seeking to ensure an unbroken flow of interest month after month. While the border peaks in summer, its season extends seamlessly from April into October. As early as March there was colour and form from groupings such as dark green *Pinus mugo* framed by the orangey-green leaf spikes of the New Zealand *Libertia*

peregrinans, which are at their brightest in the cold. At summer's end, the gap left as the achilleas and giant silvery heads of *Allium cristophii* faded was filled in by hydrangeas and cardoons coming into play. Christo compared the border to a closely woven tapestry, and was adamant that from the end of May no bare earth should be visible.

In the introduction to his book devoted to the subject, *Succession Planting* (2005), Christo asserts that one of the principal aims of today's gardener is to give year-round pleasure 'by keeping the show going over as long a period as possible'. The mixed border, he argued, with its range of different plant types, offers the greatest potential to fulfill this aim. He advised readers to use shrubs for reliable structure and solidity: among his own favourite anchor plants were variegated *Euonymus fortunei* 'Silver Queen' and evergreen aucubas. Then add herbaceous plants for dynamism, using annuals or biennials to fill gaps as perennials finish flowering or die down. Grasses offer contrast (but are rather dull in themselves, Christo thought) and bedding contributes splashes of colour. Climbers he considered versatile, as they can be trailed to cover low patches or trained up tall supports to draw the eye skywards. And through it all, self-

Above: Dramatic forms rise above the enclosing hedges in the Exotic Garden. The Japanese banana plants (*Musa basjoo*) are not brought in for winter, but are wrapped in a protective layer of straw and left in place.

sowers provide a thread of continuity as well as ensuring a refreshing blast of originality and improvisation – although Christo felt they needed 'the strictest control'.

Gradually Christo went to make other changes at Dixter. In the Peacock Garden, he replaced the lavender hedges (which had struggled in the heavy clay soil) with lines of *Aster lateriflorus* var. *horizontalis*. This dense, sturdy, low-growing plant forms a shrub-like hedge, fizzing with tiny purple-white florets in autumn and retaining its shape until spring, when it is cut back. At this point the blue *Iris latifolia* emerge, providing architectural shoots which flower in midsummer and die back just as the aster is coming back into its own. Christo also embellished the High Garden, where espaliered fruit trees and narrow flower borders screened the vegetable plots in typical Edwardian fashion. Here he added some of the nursery stock, transforming even this utilitarian area into a delightful pleasure garden.

In the Sunk Garden, Christo removed Daisy's crab apple trees. He had always resented them for their shapelessness, their brief season of beauty and the meanness of their fruit. In their place he planted *Osmanthus delavayi*, a neat evergreen shrub that can be clipped to provide architectural impact,

RHUBARB AND GINGER STEAMED SPONGE PUDDING from *GARDENER COOK*

This quantity serves four

250g/½lb rhubarb, cut into 3–4cm/1½in pieces
3 tablespoons syrup from preserved stem ginger
125g/4oz butter
125g/4oz Demerara sugar
grated rind of one orange
2 eggs, separated
125g/4oz fresh breadcrumbs
1 teaspoon ground ginger
35g/1oz preserved stem ginger, chopped
a little milk (if needed)

Butter a 1 litre/2 pint (or, for comfort, 1.5 litre/2½ pint) pudding basin. Put the stem ginger syrup in the bottom, then add the chopped rhubarb. Cream the butter with the Demerara sugar and grated orange rind. Beat in the egg yolks. Fold in the breadcrumbs and ground ginger. Mix in the stem ginger, adding a little milk if the mixture is too stiff. Fold in the egg whites, whisked till stiff. Transfer to the basin, cover with a double layer of foil and steam for two hours. Turn out and serve with custard or cream.

its fragrant spring flowers scenting the air for weeks. Christo also removed the bearded irises with which Nathaniel had filled the corners of the Sunk Garden. Although they were one of Daisy's favourite plants, Christo could not forgive their habit of looking bedraggled for most of the year, especially as they cannot be masked by neighbouring plants because their rhizomes need to bake in the summer heat. While much of the Sunk Garden was kept free of plants to retain the sense of serenity, Christo did put in clumps of New Zealand acaenas to give some interest at ground level, later adding *Canna glauca* and the giant reed *Arundo donax* for vertical contrast. He also placed cotoneasters along the walls of the Barn Garden as a framework for the self-sowing plants left to provide unexpected combinations.

A pivotal moment in Dixter's history arrived in 1972, when Daisy died at the age of ninety-one. For the past half century his mother had dominated Christo's life, but her tough, puritanical approach left little room for sentiment, let alone sentimentality. Daisy had always maintained that

Above: Christo's twin passions for food and gardening are celebrated in his 1997 book *Gardener Cook*, published by Frances Lincoln Ltd. The charmingly old-fashioned recipes, many culled from Daisy's cookery books, feature such Edwardian delights as lettuce soup, steamed gooseberry pudding, elderflower cordial and mint ice cream.

Right below: Gunnera unfolds in spring to reveal great sail-like leaves which tower over the Horse Pond by early summer.

Above: In later life Christo and Beth Chatto became great friends: they travelled, lectured and even wrote together. Letters they exchanged were published in *Dear Friend and Gardener* (1998), an engaging account of two very different gardening households. Chatto's mature family, staff and ecological garden in Essex were pitted against Christo and the vibrant circle of young friends and apprentices who encouraged his provocative horticultural exploits in East Sussex.

people make too much of money and of death, so the day after she died Christo duly drove up to Scotland to give a lecture (on hardy perennials, appropriately enough). Finding himself suddenly deprived of his major source of companionship – but also relieved of filial obligations – Christo discovered two new passions: friendship and food. Almost overnight he transformed himself from a shy, waspish loner into a generous, ebullient host. He filled the house with young assistants, apprentices, enthusiastic visitors and even strangers. It was not unknown for him to chat to couples on the train and on impulse invite them back for lunch. Dixter became famous for its jolly weekend parties full of enthusiastic horticulturists. With Daisy no longer there to oversee the kitchen, Christo taught himself to cook and was soon creating seasonal menus based on the garden's produce. These efforts reached a wider audience with the publication of *Gardener Cook* in 1997, which describes how to grow, harvest and prepare fruit, vegetables and herbs. The book was illustrated with glorious photographs by Howard Sooley, who had won acclaim for his pictures of Prospect Cottage, the garden of Christo's friend and fellow horticultural iconoclast, Derek Jarman.

The following year, Christo's publishers Frances Lincoln Ltd brought out *Dear Friend and Gardener*, an epistolary account of his friendship with author and nurserywoman Beth Chatto. Although Christo had little patience for Chatto's ecological approach to gardening, the pair had formed a fast friendship and their letters show them exchanging gossip, discussing life, observing nature and comparing notes.

One of the consequences of his new-found affability was that Christo rediscovered certain neglected parts of the garden, such

as the Horse Pond, which had become overgrown with self-seeded oaks, brambles and broom since his father's death. When Christo began entertaining, this distant corner of the garden offered a private refuge where he and his guests could retreat from the crowds of garden visitors. But it needed some attention. Once he had cleared the undergrowth to plant rhododendrons in the shade of the trees, Christo cleaned up the pond, planted water lilies in the mud at the bottom of the shallow water, then surrounded the banks with clumps of gunnera punctuated by the vertical lines of bamboo. This new water garden is where Christo and his guests would retire to with their postprandial coffee, to lounge on the grassy banks and watch the birds, fish, frogs and other pond life.

While Christo had always been fascinated by colour and form, over the years the obligation to turn out weekly articles for his various columns goaded him into experimenting with ever-more unusual plants. He tried out *Aciphylla*, the spiky New Zealand spear grass; the South American giant sea holly *Eryngium pandanifolium*, with its starry sprays; and the alpine thistle *Carlina acaulis*. The subtle colouring and architectural shapes of such plants provided structure for his dramatic borders. Christo was remarkably unsnobbish about colour: he

Above: Christo's fascination with plants was not focused solely on colour. In the garden, and as a flower arranger, he was constantly experimenting with unusual combinations, and appreciated the textures, forms and foliage of plants such as eryngium (far left) and euphorbia (middle and right) to the same extent as he did the showier flowers.

PERENNIAL PLANTING

The new perennials movement was a reaction against the neat, fussy, high-maintenance gardens of the 1980s. It introduced an open, airy, natural look, using bold drifts of herbaceous perennials and grasses chosen as much for their structure as for their colour. Although the movement came to prominence in the 1990s, its roots lie in the early twentieth century, with the work of William Robinson (1838–1935) and the German nurseryman Karl Foerster (1874–1970). The scale of the new perennial planting at Great Dixter is particularly impressive, its height and fullness relative to human scale (see right).

Above right: Daisy introduced the first meadow plantings at Great Dixter, and they have remained a major feature of the gardens. As Christo once pointed out: 'they are not just plots of grass that we gave up mowing for lack of labour, but were intended from the very first'. Orchids native to the Weald thrive in the long grass, as do daffodils, crocuses and adder's tongue ferns – the sweep of meadow forming a link with the landscape beyond.

had always shown a fondness for unorthodox combinations, such as his classic pairing of red tulips with lime-green euphorbia. Similarly, he championed such vibrant flowers as *Meconopsis* x *sheldonii* whose central boss of golden stamens provide an excellent contrast to the politely pastel blue petals. And defying the pronouncements of horticultural pundits he promoted variegated plants, often choosing variegated varieties of phormium, yucca and miscanthus. In his final book he advised his readers to guard against prejudice, especially prejudice directed at certain colours (orange) or in favour of others (blue), averring: 'there are so many restrictions on our lives that it seems a shame to impose more of them.'

In 1979 Christo's gardening genius was officially acknowledged when he received the Royal Horticultural Society's Victoria Medal of Honour, the highest horticultural accolade awarded by the Society. In the year 2000 his contribution to British horticulture would be recognized on a wider, national level when he was appointed to the OBE. By the late 1980s, however, the garden was becoming quite dense and enclosed. When the great storm of 1987 felled one of the pair of mulberry trees flanking Lutyens' circular, grass-filled steps, Christo decided not to replace it. The canopies had come to completely screen the house and he found

Right: Narrow paths and confined beds in the Exotic Garden cause the plants to burst out in an exuberant explosion. The effect is enhanced by high, enclosing hedges which also serve to screen this late-summer garden when not in season.

the backdrop of mellow red brick walls more appealing. Similarly, when the storm destroyed a row of fruit trees near the Horse Pond, Christo didn't replace them. Later he decided to turn this area into a prairie, inspired by the plants he had seen while travelling with Beth Chatto in the American Midwest. This modern trend for perennial planting was pioneered by the influential Dutch plantsman and garden designer Piet Oudolf, but it was Christo and his friend Beth who began to popularize the approach in Britain.

In 1993 Christo hired a new head gardener, Fergus Garrett, whom he had met five years earlier: Fergus had visited the garden with his class from Wye College, where he was doing a degree in horticulture. When Fergus joined Dixter, Christo was enthused with new energy. Inspired by his vibrant young accomplice, he enacted the most famous and controversial of his alterations: he grubbed up the eighty-year-old Rose Garden. This area had been badly sited from the start. Being in a trough, it was subject to winter frosts and summer heat and, in any case, the earth had gone stale and the roses were no longer thriving. Nonetheless there was outrage in the horticultural community when Christo abandoned this stalwart of English horticulture. Like a naughty child, he delighted in the furore this caused. Reporting at length on the process, he described as 'music to my ears' the sound of the rose roots being ripped from the earth.

Relieved of the constraints of tradition and taste, he could experiment at will and he decided to transform the newly emptied space into an Exotic Garden. Retaining the

Left: Rejuvenated by the arrival of Fergus Garrett as head gardener in 1993, Christo reassessed the garden and went ahead with some bold changes. The two would walk around the garden every morning to discuss, analyse and plan. In this way, by Christo's side, Fergus learnt the essence of Dixter's style.
Below: Pots grouped around the front porch allowed Christo to show off his tender plants and experiment with temporary combinations of colour and form. The bedroom above, with windows overlooking the garden on three sides, became Christo's in the later part of his life.

ten original stone-edged beds, he filled them with brightly coloured plants to create a tropical effect. The garden is not planted until June, when the earth is warm and the nights reliably frost-free, and takes until late summer to reach its zenith. This is the only section of the estate with a single season – but what a glorious season it has, as the beds overflow with jolts of colour and dramatic forms, their sheer size magnified by the narrow paths and the high, enclosing yew walls. This is an area of alpha plants: bamboos, the hardy Japanese banana (*Musa basjoo*), the giant, cane-like *Arundo donax* and elephant's ears (*Colocasia*), whose shield-shaped leaves can reach 1.5 metres/5 feet in length. Just as catholic as his mother in his choice of plant combinations, Christo was happy to interweave such exotica with mundane but colourful morning glories, and he even retained a few roses for contrast. Predictably enough, despite the initial indignation it provoked, Christo's Exotic Garden began a trend for exotic planting.

Encouraged by his new head gardener, Christo reassessed other parts of the garden and soon they made more changes. They turned the clean neat lawn around Nathaniel's chess-piece topiary into a meadow, whose soft texture created a dramatic contrast with the crisp lines of the clipped yew. Then they replaced the lawn in the Wall Garden with a more utilitarian hard surface; while flagstones may have seemed the obvious choice, Christo decided on a mosaic made from Dungeness shingle. The mosaic depicts Christo's dachshunds of the moment, Canna and Dahlia, their large eyes made of stones from Derek Jarman's garden. This new surface provided a setting for the essential late-afternoon tea, early-evening drinks and night-time digestives. It also provided additional space to feature delicate potted plants and flowers. Under Fergus' guidance as the nursery expanded, he and Christo had begun to display their treasures in tiered arrangements of clay pans and pots, massed on either side of the front porch. Here, as in the borders, they could experiment with striking,

Above: Framed in the arch of the medieval porch, the latest pair of dachshunds continues the tradition of animating the garden, guarding the house and marshalling the visitors.
Left: It was Christo's view that 'the basis of good gardening must always be a love of plants.' He was an advocate of the mixed border, where shrubs, bulbs, perennials, grasses and any other plants he liked could combine to form a satisfying and closely woven tapestry over many months.

clashing, strident and unexpected combinations, from early spring bulbs to late-autumn nerines.

For fifteen years Fergus worked alongside Christo, reaping his wisdom, learning his techniques, adopting and adapting his style, rather as Christo had apprenticed with Daisy half a century before. Every morning Christo and Fergus would spend an hour walking around the garden, creating a shortlist of immediate tasks and a longer-term list. Unlike many previous Dixter apprentices and head gardeners, who boarded with Christo or lodged in outlying cottages, Fergus chose to move into the nearby town of Hastings with his wife and two children. So in 2005 when Christo was due to have an operation on his knees, the New Zealander Aaron Bertelsen, a gardening friend, returned from the Jerusalem Botanical Gardens to live in the house and help. And when Christo died of a stroke in 2006, Fergus was the natural successor to the garden while Aaron continued as house manager, tending to Dixter's furnishings, visitors and guests.

Understandably reluctant to dwell on future plans for Dixter, Christo initially veered between letting the garden disappear and preserving it. He was loath to bequeath it to the National Trust, which he felt would preserve it in aspic, and there was insufficient money to provide the endowment that the National Trust required to accept a property. In the end Christo set up the Great Dixter Charitable Trust to ensure that the garden would carry on beyond his lifetime, offering inspiration to gardeners, apprentices and students.

Today, Dixter continues to evolve, and the garden begins to reflect Fergus' influence. While the details change, however, the spirit of Dixter lives on. The garden still revels in unusual plants and unorthodox combinations, but is cooler, softer and more subtle than in Christo's day. Umbellifers and perennial grasses contribute a light, airy feel; self-sown plants, which were always tolerated, are now welcomed. Informal plants like cow parsley thread their way through the borders, uniting garden spaces and enhancing the natural effect. Students, apprentices and visiting horticulturists inhabit the house and various cottages. And the garden is still full of surprises.

BETH CHATTO'S GARDEN IN ESSEX

In the 1960s Beth Chatto began to garden on wasteland which had been deemed unfit for farming. Drawing on ecological principles – choosing the right plant for the right conditions – she turned the disadvantages of the site into virtues and created a rich, varied garden full of unexpected plants and unusual combinations. On the thin dry soil near the house she placed Mediterranean plants such as cistus, salvias, euphorbias and verbascum. In the valley, she dammed up a spring to create a series of ponds, planted with lush marginal and water plants, ferns, gunnera, hostas and water irises. She planted the woodland with shade-loving bulbs and ground cover and, in the former car park, created a gravel garden of drought-tolerant plants such as alliums, grasses and lavenders. These receive no artificial irrigation even though the rainfall in this region, about 60 centimetres/24 inches per annum, is among the lowest in Britain. Through her writings and her nursery, Beth Chatto has inspired a generation of ecologically minded gardeners.

SCOTNEY CASTLE & LANNING ROPER

This romantic woodland was created around the ruins of a medieval moated castle. Designed according to picturesque principles, it provides dramatic, framed views which celebrate the ancient architecture while drawing in the surrounding slopes. These are planted with kalmia, magnolias, rhododendrons and azaleas for spring colour, followed by summer-flowering roses and wisteria. A romantic precursor to the wild gardens of William Robinson, Scotney is a nineteenth-century example of the move towards an informal, natural style. In the 1960s Lanning Roper designed a herb garden for the forecourt of the old castle, and when the property was later bequeathed to the National Trust, he advised on the restoration of the estate.

Left top: In her Essex garden, Beth Chatto transformed an abandoned wasteland into a horticultural paradise by carefully choosing plants to suit each specific site. Pioneering an 'ecological planting' approach, her garden has an exotic quality as it groups plants from a wide range of countries which enjoy the same growing conditions.

Left below: Like its near neighbour, Great Dixter, Scotney Castle was created around the ruins of a moated medieval manor house. The horticultural exuberance of the picturesque-style gardens was an early inspiration to Christo, who used to visit with his mother.

Above: Prospect Cottage, the garden of film-maker Derek Jarman, whose 'found art' echoes the vertical towers of the Dungeness Nuclear Power Station looming in the distance.

DEREK JARMAN'S PROSPECT COTTAGE

This is the tiny fisherman's cottage where the iconoclastic film-maker, writer and artist Derek Jarman created a small but very influential garden, on a bleak, shingle beach in the shadow of the Dungeness nuclear power station. Using endemic, salt-tolerant plants he made a formal space in front, with symmetrical beds and clusters of stones, while behind he made a sculpture garden of found objects – flotsam washed up on the beach and redeployed as art. Poetry is also present, in the verses of John Donne's *The Sun Rising* transcribed on the side of the cottage. Jarman drew much inspiration from Great Dixter, which he praised for its shagginess: 'If a garden isn't shaggy, forget it.' His own garden, in turn, inspired a fashion for extreme horticulture as people sought increasingly alien and inauspicious sites in which to attempt to create new gardens. It also fostered a trend for maritime gardens, demonstrating the range of plant material – kale, lychnis, sedum, poppies and gorse, as well as dog roses, carnations, valerian and fennel – capable of growing in shingle. Jarman began creating the garden soon after he was diagnosed as HIV-positive. It was to be his final and most enduring art work – a horticultural gesture of faith which has become a place of pilgrimage for garden-makers and non-gardeners alike.

INDEX

Page numbers in *italics* indicate a caption to an illustration; page numbers in **bold** indicate a boxed entry.

GARDEN CONTACT DETAILS

Stowe, Buckingham, Buckinghamshire, MK18 5EQ
www.nationaltrust.org.uk/stowe/.

Biddulph Grange, Grange Road, Biddulph, Staffordshire, ST8 7SD
www.nationaltrust.org.uk/biddulph-grange-garden/.

Nymans, Handcross, near Haywards Heath, West Sussex, RH17 6EB
www.nationaltrust.org.uk/nymans/.

Great Dixter, Northiam, Rye, East Sussex TN31 6PH
www.greatdixter.co.uk/.

PHOTOGRAPHIC ACKNOWLEDGMENTS

t = top; b = bottom; l = left; r = right; c = centre; r1–5 = timeline

Commissioned photography by Nathan Harrison as follows: 2, 4, 6, 44–45, 46, 47, 50, 52, 54–55, 57b, 58, 59, 60t, 61, 62 (all), 63, 64 (all), 66, 69, 70, 73, 74–5, 76, 77, 78–9, 80, 81, 85, 90–91, 93, 105, 109 (all), 110t, 111 (all), 112–3, 114 (all), 115 (all), 117, 118–9, 120bl & br, 121, 122, 123, 124, 125 (all), 126, 127, 129, 134, 138–9, 140, 144, 149 (all), 150 (all), 151, 152, 156–7, 162b, 163, 164–5, 166t, 166b, 175, 176, 177b, 180–81, 183, 192–3, 196, 201, 203, 204–5, 206, 207, 209b, 210 (all), 211, 215, 216 (all), 217.

Country Life: 162t.

CORBIS: 28.

David Ross/Britain Express: 9b.

GAP Photos: John Glover 17b, 219; J. S. Sira 218b; Marcus Harpur 218t; Suzie Gibbons 147b.

Jonathan Buckley: 182, 212.

judywhite/gardenphotos.com: 35.

Harpur Garden Pictures: 209t.

Hatfield House: 27.

National Portrait Gallery: 53.

Rodtuk: 86.

Victoria and Albert Museum: 24, 104t.

National Media Museum/Science & Society Picture Library: 135b.

National Trust Image Library: 56t, 56b, 57t, 68, 82, 83, 84, 89, 94t, 107, 108, 116b, 128, 132t, 132b, 155, 160b, 173, 177t.

RHS Lindley Library: 16t, 32, 36t, 36br, 39, 42, 60b, 71, 92, 135t, 145l, 145r, 147t, 153, 158, 168, 169c, 169l, 169r, 170, 187, 197b.

Nymans: 143, 148, 154tl, 154tr, 154b, 160t, 161, 167, 171t, 172.

Great Dixter: 184t, 184b, 185, 186tr, 186tr, 186b, 188t, 188b, 190, 191, 194, 195, 197t, 198, 199t, 199b, 200, 214, 189.

Shutterstock: Acambium64 11tl; Andy Lidstone 12b; Antonio Abrignani 13r2; Chad Bontrager 14b; David Hughes 178t; Debu55y 88; Diana Taliun 11br; freya–photographer 36bl; Georgios Kollidas 21r1, 21r2, 21r4, 35r5, 37; Hein Nouwens 1; irisphoto1 13r4; Jamesdavidphoto 31; JeniFoto 9r3; John Copland 9r4; Kamira 9r1; Khirman Vladimir 9t; Lance Bellers 137t; Lasse Kristensen 208; Madlen 18, 23, 40b; MarkauMark 35r1; Morphart Creation 110b; mountainpix 10; Neftali 20; Nicku 131; Niek Goossen 178b; Papik 11bl; Pete Spiro 40t; Pieter Stander 179; Rachelle Burnside 22b; Radiocat endpapers; rook76 16b; Skowronek 137b; stocker1970 87; Teri Virbickis 9r5; Texturis 11tr; Wallenrock 202; Zvonimir Atletic 13r3.